FOUR AGES OF MAN

FOUR AGES OF MAN

The Classical Myths

BY JAY MACPHERSON

I'll tell ye, 'tis not vain, nor fabulous
(Though so esteem'd by shallow ignorance),
What the sage Poets taught by the heav'nly Muse
Storied of old in high immortal verse
Of dire Chimaeras and enchanted Isles,
And rifted Rocks whose entrance leads to hell,
For such there be, but unbelief is blind.

MILTON

1965

THE MACMILLAN COMPANY OF CANADA LIMITED

TORONTO

Reprinted July 1962

Reprinted November 1963

Reprinted February 1965

PRINTED IN CANADA

FOREWORD

This book is organized chronologically, in four phases: creation and the coming of the gods; pastoral life and the ordering of the seasons; the adventures and the labours of the heroes; war, tragic tales, and decline into history. This scheme corresponds very roughly to that of the classical Four Ages – hence the title. The title is intended to suggest that myths are ordinarily told in a sequence which, though not strictly historical, has some analogy to history. Some of the details of this analogy are indicated in the chart at the end.

Grateful acknowledgement for permission to reproduce the illustrations which appear on the pages indicated is made to the following: the executors of the late Sir Arthur Evans (for the illustrations on pages 89 and 95 which are taken from *The Palace of Minos* by Sir Arthur Evans); the Museum of Fine Arts, Boston (page 40); the Metropolitan Museum of Art, Rogers Fund, 1910 (page 115); the Journal of Hellenic Studies (pages 134 and 138); the Journal of Hellenic Studies and the British Museum (page 14); the Syndics of the Cambridge University Press (page 96, from *Zeus* by A. B. Cook; and pages 6, 67, 102, 105, 112, from *Prolegomena to the Study of Greek Religion* by J. E. Harrison).

My warmest thanks are due to Kildare Dobbs, who suggested it; to Hope Arnott Lee, who encouraged and advised; to Clive Parsons, who dispelled difficulties and made it presentable; and to Northrop Frye, without whom as always not.

J. M.

CONTENTS

FOUR AGES OF MAN

INTRODUCTION

"MYTH" is a Greek word meaning story, especially a story about gods or heroes. We do not know exactly when and how these stories began to be told, but they come into literature first of all in the works of the early Greek poets Homer and Hesiod. The Greeks had no Bible, or single collection of sacred writings. Their sacred stories are not fixed in a single written version like those of the Jews, but are continually reshaped by later poets and dramatists. Disputes arise about what the stories mean, whether they are "true" and if so in what sense; but they keep on being told, whatever different hearers may make of them.

Some generations later than Homer, when people began not just to tell the stories but also to ask what they "really" meant, the answers they found were of different kinds. Some thought that the gods and heroes were mortal men remembered after their death for remarkable deeds and gradually coming to be thought of as more than human – in other words, that the myths were really history. Others thought they were a kind of natural science: that Zeus the father-god did not just

Illustration: Sea-god

1

live in the sky but was the sky itself, and his wife Hera the air. Another kind of interpretation is moral, making the stories into examples of how the good man should behave. Here the hero's enemies all represent vices and temptations.

We have to remember that the myths are not all of the same kind, or even of the same age, and no one explanation will fit them all. Some do seem to refer to historical events. For example, though most of the Greek myths are about Zeus and his family, all the Greek writers know that before these "younger gods" arrived there were older generations of gods. When we are told that Zeus seized the throne of Heaven from his father Cronus, or that Apollo took over the shrine at Delphi from the earth-goddess, the stories suggest vague memories of how an older religion was displaced by a new one. Myths in which Greek heroes perform great actions in Troy, Crete and Egypt remind us of those rich and powerful Mediterranean empires that were already in decline before Greek civilization arose.

Another view of the myths as history, which we might call anthropological, sees in some often-repeated incidents facts of primitive social life and ritual, perhaps glossed over or not understood by the story-teller. The classical Greeks sacrificed animals to the gods, but certainly not human beings. But stories in which a youth or maiden connected with the fruitfulness of the earth dies or is carried away suggest that possibly the Greeks' remote ancestors put young human victims to death to ensure the yearly harvest. Again, the reader will be struck by the number of kings, in heaven as on earth, who try to make away with their children for fear of being supplanted by them. In many prehistoric societies, and very likely in early Greece as well, an ageing king would be killed by his successor before his strength began to decline, for the good of his people and the land.

We shall find also in the myths some explanations of natural events. Mount Etna in Sicily is a volcano because the dreadful monster Typhon is buried under it; his anger shakes the ground, and he vomits forth fire and molten rock. The Great Bear never sets into the western sea because the god of Ocean is angry with her. The earth is barren for half the year because the corn-mother Demeter is mourning for her daughter, the spring-maiden Persephone, hidden beneath the ground.

As for moral explanations, they are much harder to prove. A few of the myths can be told so as to bring out examples of virtue or the truths of religion, but it is doubtful that their first tellers thought of them in that way. Many of them, especially those in which the gods cheat, lie, kidnap and seek vengeance, could hardly offer worse models of conduct. At the same time, we frequently meet figures who bear the names of moral or spiritual qualities: Metis (Counsel), Prometheus and Epimetheus (Forethought and Afterthought), Cupid and Psyche (Love and the Soul), and whose stories suggest allegorical or "deeper" meanings.

It was not until late in the classical age that the most remarkable thing about the myths began to be discovered. By then the altars of the Greek and Roman gods were cold: Christianity had replaced their worship. Readers of the Bible and of other eastern literatures began to see striking resemblances between the myths of the Greeks and those of other peoples: a discovery both exciting and perplexing. Christian readers recognized familiar themes in the garden of the Hesperides, where a serpent twines about a marvellous tree; the destruction done to mankind by an apple and a woman, or by that other "all-gifted" woman with her fatal curiosity; Deucalion's flood; the dividing-up of the world among three brothers; a maiden sacrificed by her father; a hero, born of a god and a mortal woman, who triumphs over death. Many explanations for such similarities were offered. Some thought that these were stories of the devils who ruled the world before Christ came into it and overthrew their power; others, that they were parodies of the truth put about by demons to lead the faithful astray. A more charitable view made them fragmentary and shadowy accounts of the truths that God revealed fully only in the Bible: thus Christians might read these fables of the heathen poets without harm and perhaps even with some profit.

In our own day explanations are still being sought for the similarities that exist among the myths of all peoples. Did all cultures take their rise from a single source – some Mesopotamian or ancient Indian valley? an Atlantis long gone under the western sea? perhaps the dark continent of Africa, or the still mysterious North? It may be a question for psychology: does the human imagination work by laws that are the same everywhere, producing the same stories again and again from the common materials of life – day and night, seed-time and harvest, fear, desire, and rest?

Whatever explanations we may give for their continuing power, these stories, among the oldest in the world, are still among the best. They have been so important to writers from Homer right down to the present that we can no more study literature without them than we can without the Bible, the fountain-head of Jewish and Christian tradition. Their meaning has been transformed from generation to generation and from writer to writer, but the old patterns and characters survive.

Myth is the most ancient kind of story-telling; and these tales from ancient Greece and Rome, along with those of the Bible and the later European folk-tales like those collected in Germany by the brothers Grimm, remain the basis of our fiction. There are really very few stories, as we must all have thought at the movies. Or rather, there are any number of stories, but they are all based on a few kinds of plot: narratives of creation, transformation and destruction, of love, loss, revenge, of friendship and conflict, of quest and disappointment and success. There are also only a few basic settings: the heavenly world above the clouds, the underworld, and between them our own earth, whether paradisal and unspoiled or ravaged by greed, pride and war. Myth makes far more use than modern fiction does of celestial and infernal settings, and its characters are mainly either gods or heroes with lesser but still superhuman powers. Apart from science-fiction, which often seems startlingly close to fairy-tale and myth, most modern novels and films are set firmly in the ordinary world and deal with characters whose powers are limited like our own. Nevertheless, in many the old patterns can still be traced out. The cruel father, the helpless princess, the brave rescuer, the child of mysterious origin, the wise old prophet, the curse, the quest, the fatal treasure – these may take as many forms as the shape-changing Old Man of the Sea, but like him they are indestructible, and like him they can tell the one who holds them fast something of where he is going and what he is.

I. IN THE BEGINNING

THE CREATION

> *In the beginning how the heavens and earth*
> *Rose out of Chaos . . .*

MILTON

IN THE beginning, before the heavens and the earth, all there was was Chaos, the dark and formless void. And after ages of time had passed, there appeared two tremendous beings, the most ancient goddess Night and her brother Erebus, the Depth. And from these two was born Eros, who is Love, the most powerful of all the gods. After him arose Gaia, the great Earth-Mother, who brought forth from herself first the world we live on and then Uranus, the starry sky, that lies above and around her and is the eternal home of the blessed gods. Then

Illustration: Eros

subtle Eros brought the Earth-Mother and the Sky-Father together in love, and from them in the course of time were born a series of strange and monstrous creatures, the early births of time. First came the three brothers Gyes, Cottus and Briareos, huger than mountains, fifty-headed and hundred-handed, terrifying to look upon. So at least thought their father Uranus, and he took them from their mother and shut them up in the dark places under the earth. Gaia next bore the three Cyclopes, the Wheel-Eyed ones, smaller than the Hundred-Handed but still giants, and each having a single round eye in the centre of his forehead. These too their father shut away in the earth, afraid less of their size and strength than of their skill at forging metal weapons, for they were the first smiths.

The last children of Gaia were the twelve Titans, six sons and six daughters, larger than mortal men but not monstrous, endowed with beauty and majesty. Then Gaia, weary of Uranus' cruel treatment of her other children, appealed to her Titan sons to avenge their sufferings. She offered them a sharp sickle of adamant, the hardest of stones, with which to wound their father and drive him away. Only Cronus, the youngest and bravest, dared attempt such a deed. He waited until night fell and Uranus came down to embrace Gaia; then he took the sickle and maimed his father, severing the embrace of Earth and Sky. Then Cronus ruled in his father's place over the whole world; but he would not release his monstrous elder brothers from their captivity under the earth.

The six Titan brothers took their six sisters for wives, and their progeny were the gods that fill the land and sea and air. To his oldest brother Oceanus, Cronus gave the stream that girdles the earth, and his children were the deities of the water. His innumerable sons were the Rivers of the earth, and his daughters were the Nymphs of fountain, lake and stream, as well as of the sea. The Nymphs are a gentle and kindly race, beloved by gods and men; but one of them, whose name is Styx, the Hateful, is unlike the others. Her stream rises in a sunless underground cavern and her waters are chill and numbing to the heart. Even the gods if they swear by Styx fear to break their oath.

The most beautiful of Uranus' Titan children were the light-god Hyperion and his sister-wife Thea, who lived in a palace of clouds in the eastern sky and whose children were Helios the Sun, Selene the Moon, and Eos the Dawn. Eos became the mother of Phosphorus the Morning Star, Hesperus the Evening Star, and the Planets, the wandering stars. Her other children are Eurus, Zephyrus, Notus, and Boreas, the Four Winds that blow from east, west, south and north.

THE GOLDEN AGE

> *For during Saturn's ancient reign it's said*
> *That all the world with goodness did abound:*
> *All lovèd virtue, no man was afraid*
> *Of force, nor fraud in wight was to be found:*
> *No war was known, no dreadful trumpet's sound,*
> *Peace universal reigned mongst men and beasts,*
> *And all things freely grew out of the ground:*
> *Justice sate high adored with solemn feasts,*
> *And to all people did divide her dread behests.*
>
> SPENSER

The long reign of Cronus, whom the Romans called Saturn, was the happy time that the poets call the Golden Age. It was then that men came into being, formed from earth mixed with rain-water by Prometheus, the wise son of the Titan Iapetus. He made them in the image of the gods, unlike the animals, standing erect and looking up to heaven. In those days the whole earth was a paradise, a land of eternal spring like the dwellings of the gods. The earth brought forth its produce without man's labour and unwounded by his sharp ploughshares; the rivers ran with milk and nectar, and honey-dew dripped from the bitter oak. The animals lived at peace with one another and with man, and man was at peace with his neighbour. Metals and precious stones slept undisturbed in the ground; there was no war, no commerce, and no need for courts of law.

The men of the Golden Age lived innocently, honouring the gods, and they died peacefully without sickness or creeping age. There were as yet no women on the earth, and so the good race passed away without leaving children; but their spirits inhabit the middle air between earth and heaven and watch in love and benevolence over the righteous, blessing their flocks and fields. After they had gone, loss and change began to enter the world, which now endured progressively worse ages, the Silver, the Brazen, and the harsh Age of Iron. In the Silver Age began the four seasons as we know them, with their succession of heat and cold. In those days men began to build shelters and to sow corn in the ground, harnessing bullocks to the yoke. The men of the Silver Age were foolish and impious, and Zeus, Cronus' successor, destroyed them because they would not honour the gods. Then he created a third race, the men of bronze, who cared for nothing but warfare and died by their own violence. Last came the present race, the men of iron; these too in their turn shall Zeus destroy, say the poets.

WAR IN HEAVEN

> *Who stands secure? Are even Gods so safe?*
> *Jupiter that just now is dominant —*
> *Are there not ancient dismal tales how once*
> *A predecessor reigned ere Saturn came,*
> *And who can say if Jupiter be last?*
>
> BROWNING

When Cronus drove away his father, Uranus had cursed him, saying that he should in turn be overthrown by his own children. Through all the long years of his happy reign, this remembrance troubled Cronus and disturbed his peace. Every time his wife Rhea bore him a child, he took it from her and swallowed it, in order to defeat the prophecy. After he had swallowed in this way her first five children, Hestia, Demeter, Hera, Hades and Poseidon, Rhea resolved that the sixth child should escape the fate of the others, and she went for counsel to her mother Earth. On Earth's advice, she hid herself from Cronus in a cave of Mount Ida on the island of Crete, where she was delivered of a male child, whom she called Zeus. She left him with the Nymphs of the mountains to be nursed, and returned to Cronus. With her she brought a large smooth stone from the mountain-side, and this she wrapped in swaddling-bands and gave to Cronus, telling him that this was the latest-born of her sons. Cronus, suspecting nothing, swallowed the stone as he had done his children.

Meanwhile the infant Zeus grew and flourished, nursed by the good Nymphs and by a stranger foster-mother, the silky-white she-goat Amalthea who gave him milk and played with him. There is a story that one day the little god grasped her horn too roughly and broke it off. He immediately made a new one grow in its place, and the old horn he gave to the Nymphs in thanks for their care, promising that they should always find it full of whatever foods they most wished for, fruit and grain and honey and every other good thing. The Nymphs treasured the gift of Zeus, which was called the Horn of Plenty (Latin, *cornucopia*).

The other friends of Zeus in the Cretan cave were a band of armed youths called the Curetes, warriors born from the earth, who entertained him with leaping dances, clashing their spears against their shields when necessary to drown the noise of his crying, for fear Cronus should hear it from his high palace.

When Zeus had come to manhood, Gaia sent to him Metis, "Counsel", one of the daughters of Oceanus, who told him the time had come for him to avenge the wrongs done by his father. Acting on her instructions, he came to Cronus' golden palace, where he introduced himself as a stranger. When Cronus was far gone in wine, Zeus slipped into his cup a powerful herb that Metis had given him from Earth. No sooner had Cronus swallowed it than he vomited up first Rhea's stone, then his five elder children, all now full-grown. His brothers Hades and Poseidon joined to help Zeus bind their father in chains; but Cronus called aloud for his Titan brothers, who came running to attack the young intruders. The younger gods, seeing the Titans advancing on them, fled out of heaven to the top of Mount Olympus above the clouds, where they gathered their forces for the war that must follow.

For ten years war was waged between the younger gods and the Titans, and still the issue hung undecided. Finally Zeus, weary of the useless struggle, set out to consult the wisdom of Mother Earth at her mysterious oracle in the Pythonian cave. The words that came to him were clear, but their meaning was obscure: "Let him who would conquer in the war first set free those imprisoned in Tartarus." Zeus knew nothing of the events that had taken place in heaven before he was born, nor did he know that Gaia still hated Cronus for leaving her elder children in captivity, so he was puzzled by her message.

It happened that among the Titans there was one, the wise Prometheus, who would not fight on the side of the elder gods. He of all the living saw deepest into the secrets of time, and he knew that the reign of Cronus was running out and would soon give place to that of the Olympians. First he tried unsuccessfully to persuade his father and brothers to lay down their arms. Then, rather than fight against them himself, he came to Zeus and offered to interpret to him the oracle of Earth. When Zeus understood all that had gone before, he descended with Prometheus to the underworld, soon reaching the gate of brass-walled Tartarus, the dreadful place where Gaia's monstrous children lay imprisoned. The entrance was guarded by a she-serpent, which Zeus killed. He brought the Cyclopes back to the upper world to help him against the Titans, and the Hundred-Handed with them, but only after he had made them swear to go and live beyond the farthest bounds of the ocean, so terrifying was their destructive power.

The Cyclopes immediately set up a smithy in the depths of Etna the Sicilian volcano; and the sky above soon flared red as they hammered out gifts for their friend Zeus and his brothers. To the eldest, Poseidon, they gave a trident with three sharp prongs of adamant; to the second, Hades, a helmet of invisibility; and to Zeus himself, the thunderbolts that tear through all resistance and make him dreaded by gods and men. It is on this tremendous weapon that his power mainly rests, and he alone has the secret and the use of it.

Armed with their three gifts, the Olympians once more advanced to the assault on heaven. This time they were crushingly successful: the Titans could not stand against the new weapons, but fled thunder-scarred out over the battlements and plunged into the depths below. The Olympians pursued them, giving all they captured into the charge of the Hundred-Handed, who stowed them away in those very underworld caverns from which they themselves had just been released. A remnant of the Titanic forces, Cronus and a few followers, got away to a high mountain in Northern Greece, where they held out for a time, sheltering in caves from the dreaded thunderbolts; but at last they were routed out of this stronghold and fled away over the sea, finding a haven, some say, in sunny Italy before the Romans were ever thought of. Others say that the hunted king came to rest only among the mists and glooms of Britain, far on the ocean's remotest verge. No stories tell his end.

In the last flight one prisoner was taken: Atlas, a brother of Prometheus, a giant of great strength. Zeus ordained as his punishment that he should stand at the western edge of the world bearing on his shoulders the weight of the sky. No wonder his name is thought to mean "he who suffers".

THE REIGN OF ZEUS

> *At Heaven's door*
> *Look in, and see each blissful deity*
> *How he before the thunderous throne doth lie,*
> *Listening to what unshorn Apollo sings*
> *To the touch of golden wires, while Hebe brings*
> *Immortal nectar to her kingly sire.*
> MILTON

Zeus and his brothers ruled earth and Mount Olympus together, and they cast lots for the rest of the world. Zeus won for his share the air and sky, from which he takes his title of Cloud-gatherer. Poseidon the Earth-shaker rules the sea, and Hades the dark realms under the earth. Besides being the sky-god, Zeus was the guardian of law and order on earth, upholding fatherly and kingly authority and protecting travellers and guests. Of his sisters, the most famous is his queen

Hera, the patron of marriage. Another, Hestia, was the
guardian of the sacred fire in heaven and of the hearth, the
centre of family worship, in homes on earth.

Most of the other Olympian gods were children of Zeus.
An earlier wife of his was his adviser, the goddess Metis.
Fearing the prophecy that one of his children would one day
overthrow him in his turn, he took the precaution of swallow-

Throned Zeus

ing Metis, whose daughter Athene when she was ready to be
born sprang out through the top of her father's head. Some
say she was wearing full armour at the time. Athene was a
warrior-maiden, the patroness of Athens, and she inherited
her mother's wisdom.

Jealous of Zeus' having apparently produced a child all by
himself, Hera, calling on Earth to help her, brought forth a
son without a father, the smith-god Hephaestus. But Hephaestus was born lame, and his mother in disgust threw him out

of heaven. Or, as another story has it, he took his mother's side in a quarrel with Zeus, who threw him over the heavenly threshold. All day from morning to night he fell, until he struck earth on the island of Lemnos, where after he recovered he built an underground forge. Later he was gladly welcomed back into heaven, on account of his marvellous skill. Another of Hera's children was the goddess Hebe, the cup-bearer at the celestial feasts.

Phoebus Apollo and the huntress Artemis were Zeus' children by the Titaness Leto, who before their birth fled all over the Mediterranean looking for a place where she could escape the jealous anger of Hera. The island of Delos offered her shelter, but even then Hera would not let the birth-goddess Eileithyia go and attend her until all the other goddesses insisted. Then at last her twins were born, and Apollo built a temple on Delos as a reward for its kindness.

Hermes the swift messenger, the son of Zeus by the nymph Maia, was a tricky and precocious child. On the day of his birth he invented the lyre by stretching sinews on a frame whose base was a tortoise-shell. Then he went for a stroll in the country and drove off fifty cattle that belonged to Apollo, making them walk backwards to deceive any pursuer. Having shut them up safely, he tucked himself back into his cradle, where Apollo found him. Accused of the theft, he pretended to be too young even to know what cattle were. But Apollo was not taken in, and he would have punished the guileful baby severely if Hermes had not given him the lyre as payment for the cows. This was the first act of barter, and it established Hermes as the god of merchants as well as of thieves.

Aphrodite, the goddess of love delighting in laughter, was born from the foam of the sea near the island of Cythera and came ashore at Cyprus. Both islands remained sacred to her. She was the wife of Hephaestus, but preferred the war-god

Ares, the turbulent son of Zeus and Hera.

These twelve great Olympian gods were not the only dwellers in heaven. Zeus had a third sister, the corn-mother Demeter, who watched over the fruitfulness of the earth. A son of Zeus was the vine-god Dionysus, a graceful young man attended by a drunken old fellow, Silenus, who called himself

Aphrodite attended by the Loves

his tutor. Hermes' goat-footed, goat-horned son Pan chose to live on earth rather than in the halls of the gods. His home was in the woods and fields of Arcadia, where he played on his pipes to the nymphs and satyrs and was worshipped at rural altars as the god of shepherds and goatherds.

PROMETHEUS

> *Or, like the thief of fire from heaven,*
> *Wilt thou withstand the shock?*
> *And share with him – the unforgiven –*
> *His vulture and his rock?*
>
> BYRON

For a long time after the earth appeared, its hills and valleys and broad meadows lay untenanted, except for the nymphs and the satyrs, godlings of the countryside, who danced and played and chased one another in forest and field. We have seen already how Prometheus at last created man. A different story tells how the gods charged with the task not only Prometheus but also his brother Epimetheus. Since the name of Prometheus means "he who thinks before" and that of his brother, "he who thinks afterwards", it seems that Epimetheus did not have all his brother's wisdom. He began with the creation of the animals; and he was so lavish with the gifts he gave them – gifts of strength and speed and cunning, strong claws and sharp teeth, warm coverings of feathers and fur – that there was nothing left over for man, his poor shivering last creation. So Epimetheus called upon his wise brother to repair the mistake. Prometheus not only made man upright and beautiful, but he decided to use his craft to win extra advantages for man from Zeus, the king of the gods. Once when gods and men had met together, Prometheus cut up a great ox for them all to feast on. Dividing the body into two portions, he wrapped all the good meat up in the skin so that it looked very unappetizing, but the bones he set apart, covering them over with fat. Then he asked Zeus which portion he would take for himself and his fellow-gods. Zeus, deceived by the rich look of the glistening fat, chose with it the heap of bones that it concealed; and from then on when men killed cattle to eat, it was the bones that they sacrificed to the gods, keeping the meat for themselves.

When Zeus saw that he had been outwitted, he was angry, and in revenge he refused to give mankind the gift Prometheus wanted for them, the precious blessing of fire, but jealously guarded it in his heavenly halls. The friend of man, undaunted, went up to Olympus and stole away a flickering flame in a hollow stalk of fennel to give to the helpless race of mortals in place of the animals' strength and speed, sharp teeth and warm skins.

Then Zeus looked down from Olympus and saw everywhere on the broad earth the far-shining fires, and his anger against Prometheus knew no bounds. He sent two of his strong servants to bind him to a rock in the Caucasus Mountains, where he lay for long ages stretched out, held down by his chains, exposed alike to hot sun and fierce winds and piercing cold. To increase his torments, Zeus sent an eagle to tear continually at his liver; and because the Titan was immortal like Zeus himself, his sufferings were to be without end.

There was still a third reason for Zeus' cruelty, besides Prometheus' two victories over him. When Prometheus had helped Zeus against Cronus and the other Titans, it was not because he thought Zeus' reign would be any more just than the reigns of Cronus and Uranus before him, but because he alone of all the dwellers in heaven knew the secrets of Fate, and he saw that it was of no use to struggle against what was to come. The Fates are three sisters, Clotho, Lachesis, and Atropos, the daughters of Night, who sit in a cave spinning the thread of man's life. The first sister spins the thread, the second draws it out, and the third, the most dreaded, is she who cuts it off. Prometheus, who was admitted to their counsels, knew not only that Zeus was destined to hold the supreme power, but also that another was to come after him and seize the power in his turn. This successor was to be one of Zeus' many sons – Zeus himself knew that much: it was Prometheus who kept the crucial secret of who would be the child's mother – her name, and whether she was goddess, nymph or mortal woman. Like his father and his grandfather, Zeus lived in fear of his eventual overthrow and would have given anything to prevent it or put it off. Underestimating his old friend as he had done before, and forgetting that without Prometheus' help it would have taken him much longer to become lord of Olympus, he thought he could torture Prometheus into telling what he knew. But Prometheus with his superhuman endurance remained steadfast.

Most stories agree that at last Prometheus was released from his mountain-top. The deed is ascribed to the greatest of the heroes, Zeus' son Heracles, who sailed to his rescue in a golden cup lent to him by the Sun. Prometheus never told Zeus who was to be the mother of his destroyer, but he did warn him not to marry the sea-nymph Thetis, as his heart was set on doing, because she was destined to bear a son who would be greater than his father. Zeus prudently changed his mind and bestowed the lady on a minor hero named Peleus.

Thetis, however, had all the tricky character of her native element, and Peleus did not win her easily. He seized her one day as she slept on the seashore, whereupon she awoke in a fright and changed herself into all kinds of creatures – a bird, a tree, a tigress, a raging fire – in her struggle to escape him. But the hero held her fast, and at length she returned to her proper form and agreed to become his wife. Zeus gave the couple a famous wedding which was attended by a great throng of gods and men. Their son was Achilles, the hero of the Trojan war, a greater man than his father Peleus but a mortal like other men, not a contender for the throne of heaven.

PANDORA'S BOX

> *More lovely than Pandora, whom the gods*
> *Endowed with all their gifts; and oh! too like*
> *In sad event, when, to the unwiser son*
> *Of Japhet brought by Hermes, she ensnared*
> *Mankind with her fair looks, to be avenged*
> *On him who had stole Jove's authentic fire.*
>
> MILTON

Zeus' revenge did not stop with the punishment of Prometheus. Though he could not take the gift of fire away from
men once it had been kindled in a thousand places on the
earth, he was determined they should suffer for their possession
of it.

This story agrees with the story of the Golden Age: at first
the life of man on earth was happier than it is now, and then
miseries and discontents gradually crept in. It seems that
Prometheus and Epimetheus created men only, not women.
When Zeus was angry with mankind, he devised the worst
punishment he could think of, and invented Woman. Hephaestus, the smith of the gods, was instructed to form her from
the earth and make her irresistibly beautiful. Each of the gods
gave her his own special gift or skill, and from this she was
called Pandora, "all-gifted". When she was perfected with
every gift and arrayed in all her loveliness, this treacherous
treasure was taken down to earth by Hermes, the messenger-
god who wears winged helmet and sandals to speed his flight,
and given to Prometheus' foolish brother Epimetheus. Now
Prometheus had warned his brother not to accept anything
from Zeus, even if it looked like a gift sent in friendship; but
Epimetheus as usual acted first and thought afterwards. He
accepted the maiden from Hermes and led her into his house,
and with her a great jar – some say a box or chest – which the

gods had sent with her, telling her to keep it safely but never never think of opening it. This was too much for a lively girl like Pandora, who among her gifts was endowed with the first feminine curiosity. After restraining it for a little while, she at last gave in and lifted the lid from the jar, and from that moment began the sorrows of mankind. For each of the gods had stored in it the worst thing he was able to give, and wonderful as had been the gifts with which they endowed her, just as dreadful were the evils that rushed eagerly from the jar in a black stinking cloud like pestilent insects – sickness and suffering, hatred and jealousy and greed, and all the other cruel things that freeze the heart and bring on old age. Pandora tried to clap the lid on the jar again, but it was too late. The happy childhood of mankind had gone for ever, and with it the Golden Age when life was easy. From then on man had to wrest a hard living by his own labour from the unfriendly ground. Only one good thing came to man in the jar and remains to comfort him in his distress, and that is the spirit of Hope.

DEUCALION'S FLOOD

> ... *the ancient pair* ...
> *Deucalion and chaste Pyrrha, to restore*
> *The race of mankind drowned, before the shrine*
> *Of Themis stood devout.*
>
> MILTON

One more story is told of the early ages of the world. As time went on mankind became less and less noble, and evil and crime walked in open daylight on the face of the earth. When Cronus wounded his father Uranus, two new kinds of creature sprang from the blood where it had dripped down on the earth. One group was the three sisters called the Erinyes or Furies, terrible to look at, who track down and punish the wicked, especially those who murder their own kin. The other was the race of Giants, cruel and bloody-natured, who at last grew so arrogant that they resolved to conquer the stronghold of the gods. To do this they piled Mount Pelion on top of Mount Ossa as a base from which to reach Olympus; but when they had got that far, Zeus hurled at them one of his thunderbolts, so that the mountains came crashing down, overwhelming the Giants in their fall, and the Earth received the blood of her sons in torrents. So that they should not be forgotten, she breathed life into the blood where it had mixed with the ground, and formed a new race of men, violent and cruel in their turn. These intermarried with the race already on the earth and further corrupted their nature; and so it was that evil and crime walked abroad, while Shame and the maiden Justice departed from mankind.

The gods seeing this became greatly perturbed, and Zeus resolved to visit the earth in disguise and take a closer look. Asking here and there for hospitality as a weary traveller, he was so unkindly received that he lost patience, and hastening back to Olympus he called a council of the gods. Before all the assembled divinities of earth and sky and sea, he announced his decision to destroy mankind and replace them with a better race who would honour the gods. At first his intention was to launch a flight of thunderbolts against the earth; but remembering an old prophecy that the whole universe would eventually be consumed by fire, he laid his thunderbolts aside and chose instead to let the heavens open and destroy man with a flood. Accordingly he sent forth Notus the south wind to drive the rain out of the clouds onto the earth. At Zeus' request Poseidon called together the rivers and sent them out to break down their banks and spread themselves as far as possible over the land; then he struck the earth with his trident, and torrents of water gushed up from under the ground. The floods rushed triumphantly towards the sea, carrying before them crops and orchards, cattle and men, houses and temples, even the sacred images of the gods. Those buildings that did not collapse under the fury of the waters were overwhelmed by the high waves, and fish swam through their doorways and gazed at the rooms with their cold eyes. Soon the waters had covered everything: the whole world was sea, and sea without a shore.

At first some tried to escape by climbing the tops of hills, but the floods soon swept them away. Others took to boats, the curved keels gliding for a time above what had been homesteads and ploughed land. Beside them, for as long as they could keep up, swam all kinds of animals, wolves and sheep jostling together in their desperate efforts to escape. Birds took to the air, and wandered long in search of somewhere to rest; at last their wings grew weary and they dropped into the sea. Most of mankind was swallowed up by the waves. Even those in the boats soon died, succumbing to famine and to the sicknesses brought on by the universal stench of corruption.

In the whole world, only one spot of land still showed above the waves: the double peak of cloud-piercing Parnassus in the north of Greece. To this place after many days came floating a huge wooden chest, from which there stepped out on the dry land one man and one woman, Deucalion and his wife Pyrrha, the children respectively of Prometheus and of Epimetheus. The wisdom of Prometheus was responsible for their preservation. Knowing of Zeus' intention to destroy mankind before even Zeus himself knew it, he instructed his son and his niece and daughter-in-law to build the chest and stock it with all the provisions they would need.

Being pious people, Deucalion and Pyrrha made it their first action to give thanks to the gods for their escape. When he saw this, Zeus in pity drove back the waters with the help of Boreas the north wind, whom all this time he had kept imprisoned, and Poseidon called in all the floods he had sent out before. It was fitting that mankind should be restored from this pair, now sitting discouraged on the mountain-top; for they had kept their hands clean from the general guilt, and besides being gentle and upright they honoured the gods. Coming down from the mountain as the floods ebbed, they could see no signs of life, and felt all the horror of being the only living creatures on an empty and desolated earth. As they wandered along, they came to a temple of the goddess Themis, one of Uranus' Titan daughters who now had a place on Olympus and was worshipped beside the younger gods. Disregarding the water-weeds that slimed the steps and hung in festoons from the discoloured roof, Deucalion and Pyrrha entered the temple and implored the goddess' help and advice. After they had stood praying for a while, the voice of the goddess came to them, as if from a great distance but clearly. "Depart from my temple," it said, "veil your heads, loosen the girdles of your garments, and cast behind you the bones of your great mother." This command greatly terrified the man and his wife. Even if both their mothers were not buried far away, how could they do anything so inhuman and disrespectful? Deucalion first understood what the goddess meant. "It is Earth that is the great mother of us all, and her bones are these stones that lie on the ground." They walked away from the temple, veiled their heads, loosened their garments, and began to throw stones behind them as they walked. The stones falling to the ground lost their stiffness and hardness and began to take the form of human beings. Those Deucalion threw became men, and those Pyrrha threw became women. Ovid, the Roman poet who tells the story, explains, "So it comes about that we are a hard race, accustomed to labour, still bearing the mark of our stony origin."

PHAËTHON

> *The brotherless Heliades*
> *Melt in such amber tears as these.*
>
> MARVELL

Many years after these events, the great sun-god Helios, the son of the Titans Hyperion and Thea, came down to earth to visit a mortal woman named Clymene, the Queen of Ethiopia, a country especially dear to him; and when he went back to his palace in the sky he left her with a child. Clymene called him Phaëthon, "Shining". When he was still a young boy, being teased by his friends about having no father, Phaëthon persuaded Clymene to tell him the secret of his birth. "I swear to you," she said, "by the light above that sees me, that you are the child of that sun which you see, the sun that guides the world."

Phaëthon was eager to go immediately and seek out his great father, and Clymene instructed him how to get there. The way was not far, as the Sun's palace stood at the eastern edge of the world. By passing first through his own land of Ethiopia and then through the land of the Indians, Phaëthon was able to get there quite easily.

The palace of Helios was a wonderful structure, glittering from far off with gold and bronze that shone like fire. Inside Phaëthon discovered the great Sun sitting on his throne, in a blaze of light that made it hard to look at him. Phaëthon stood trembling and shielding his face until the Sun turned on him those eyes that see everything, and said, "My son – for I am proud to call such a young hero my child – tell me why you have come all this way to find me." Phaëthon boldly asked for some proof that he was indeed the child of Helios, and the god replied, "Ask for any gift you desire, and I shall bestow it on you. Let that hidden underground river which alone of all things my eyes have never seen, and by which the gods take their unbreakable oaths, be witness to my promise."

Then Phaëthon's pride was kindled, and he asked to be allowed for one day to drive the chariot of the Sun.

No sooner had these words been spoken than Helios repented of his oath. "My son," he said, "there is nothing I would not give to be released from my promise. You do not know what you are asking. Not one of the gods besides myself, not even mighty Zeus who hurls the thunderbolts from Mount Olympus, has the strength and skill to manage my chariot. Its fire-breathing horses are impetuous and wild, and hard enough even for me to control. Be warned in time and ask a different gift."

Burning with eager ambition, Phaëthon stood firm; and his father, sad at heart, led him out to the chariot, the work of the smith-god Hephaestus. While he was still admiring it, the moment came: Eos the dawn-goddess opened the doors of her rosy house, the stars departed, led by their shepherd the Morning Star, and the fire-breathing immortal horses of the Sun stamped in their harness. There could be no delay. Setting his son in his place, and advising him to be sure to keep to the broad middle path across the heavens, Helios let him go. Phaëthon seized the reins, gave them a shake, and was off.

As soon as they felt that an unskilled hand was guiding them and that the chariot carried less than its usual weight, the winged horses whinnied, tossed their heads, and plunged wildly about, forsaking the broad track and racing towards the highest heavens. The wretched Phaëthon was terrified when he saw how far the earth lay beneath him, and the cold stars of the northern constellations shuddered to feel the unaccustomed heat as the chariot hurtled past. Meanwhile those on earth missed the sun's friendly warmth, usually so constant, and wondered what could have happened to cause such upheaval in the heavens. The great beasts of the upper sky, Scorpion and Crab and the rest, scared the frantic driver right out of his wits; in his fright he let the reins fall from his hands, and the horses now raged entirely without control. Shying away from the highest stars, they began to dash towards the earth. Their speed scorched even the cool clouds, and the Moon as they passed was astonished to see her brother's chariot dive lower than her own.

The earth began to catch fire, starting at the mountain-tops. Where all moisture was dried out the ground split open, riven with great cracks and fissures. Meadows, crops and forests were blasted; wooded hills flamed like torches. In the fierce conflagration the skins of the Ethiopians were scorched black and Libya became a desert. Many rivers plunged underground to escape, and some have not reappeared yet: the Nile fled to the ends of the earth to hide his head, which is still hidden, leaving empty the seven channels through which he used to meet the sea.

Beholding this universal destruction, Zeus called together all the gods. With one voice they agreed, even sorrowful Helios, that if the whole earth were not to perish the desperate charioteer must be stopped. Then, mounting to the highest point of heaven, Zeus launched one of his powerful thunderbolts that always reach their mark. Cleaving the skies it struck Phaëthon and tumbled him from the chariot. With his hair on fire he fell like a comet, leaving a trail of light; at last the waters of the Italian river Po received him, far from his native land. The nymphs of Italy buried his body beside the river-shore.

There was great lamentation in the palace of Ethiopia when Phaëthon's fate was known. His sisters, also children of the Sun and called after him Heliades, were especially wild in their sorrow, until the gods pitying their distress changed them into weeping trees – poplars, from whose bark drip tears of amber to this day.

II. SPRING AND WINTER

DEMETER AND PERSEPHONE

> *... that fair field*
> *Of Enna, where Proserpin gathering flowers,*
> *Herself a fairer flower, by gloomy Dis*
> *Was gathered, which cost Ceres all that pain*
> *To seek her through the world.*
>
> MILTON

THERE was a time when the corn-mother Demeter, the sister and at the same time one of the wives of Zeus, poured out her blessings on the earth in the same abundance all the year

Illustration: Demeter, Triptolemus, Persephone

28

round. That was before her griefs estranged her from the councils of the gods.

Demeter bore a child to Zeus, the slender-ankled maiden Persephone, who grew up in surpassing beauty. When Zeus' brother Hades, the dark ruler of the underworld, asked for her in marriage, Zeus swore that he should have her, whatever her mother might say. The two brothers called in Earth to help them, and the three of them together laid a plot.

One day Persephone went to play with the daughters of Ocean in the meadows of Enna, in Sicily, away from her mother, and wandered here and there with her companions gathering the flowers of all the seasons that were blooming there together. At the will of Zeus Earth sent up from her lap a new flower, a wonderful sight for mortal men or deathless gods, a bright narcissus with a hundred blooms growing from its single stalk. The sweetness of its perfume delighted the heavens and the earth and made the sea laugh for joy. Persephone stood amazed at the flower's beauty; then as she stretched out her hand to pick it, suddenly the earth gaped, a wide chasm opened at her feet, and out of it sprang Hades in his golden chariot, drawn by deathless coal-black horses. Seizing her before she could find the power to move, he set her in his chariot and drove the horses forward.

As long as Persephone could still see the earth and the broad sky and the sea with its crowding fish, she was calm and quiet. But when the tall gates of Hades' realm came in sight and earth seemed to be lost behind her, she gave a shrill cry, so that the heights of the mountains and the depths of the sea rang with her immortal voice. Her father Zeus heard her, sitting in his temple receiving the offerings of men, and rejoiced that his design had been carried out. Her mother Demeter heard her, and the cry filled her heart with grief and fear. She rent her head-dress apart with her hands, and casting over her shoulders a dark-blue cloak, she hastened like a wild bird in search of her child, over the firm ground and the unstable sea. But there was no one who was willing to tell her the truth, even among those who knew it. For nine days and nights majestic Demeter searched over the earth, with flaming torches in her hands, so grieved that she would neither partake of the food of the gods nor refresh her body with water.

On the tenth day the dark goddess Hecate approached her, with a torch in her hand, saying, "Lady Demeter, who brings on the season and bestows good gifts, who of heavenly gods or mortal men has stolen away Persephone and pierced your heart with sorrow? For I heard her voice as she cried out, but I did not see the event."

Together Hecate and Demeter approached the sun-god Helios, who watches the doings of both gods and men. Standing before his horses, Demeter asked him whether he had seen the theft of her child. Helios replied to her, "Queen Demeter, daughter of Rhea, I pity you in your grief for your slim-ankled daughter. One alone of all the deathless gods is to blame, and that is cloud-gathering Zeus, who gave her to his brother to wife; and Hades it was who seized her, and took her in his chariot despite her loud cries down to his kingdom of mist and gloom. But, goddess, cease your lamenting: the divine ruler of a third part of the world is not an unfitting husband for your child." So saying, he hastened on with his horses, urging them forward to make up for the time he had lost.

At Helios' words the grief in Demeter's heart became more terrible and savage, and she was so angry with Zeus that she forsook the assemblies of the gods and the high places of Olympus, wandering unknown among the cities and fields of men; and during the whole time of her mourning, the seed remained hidden in the ground and the new leaves and sprouts remained closed in the plants, so that no new crop came in response to men's labours.

At last Demeter came to Eleusis, ruled over by King Celeus,

and she sat down in her distress by a well outside the town, looking like an old and weary woman. There the four daughters of Celeus met her when they came out to draw water. Not recognizing the goddess, they asked her who she was and why she did not come into the town in search of hospitality. Then Demeter, to explain why she had come alone to a strange city, told them that she had been carried away by pirates from her native Crete and had only now escaped. "But take pity on me, maidens, and tell me to what house I may go to find work suitable to my age. I can nurse a newborn child, and keep house, and supervise the women in their work."

The eldest of the daughters of Celeus replied, "None of the women who run the households of our town would send you away if you came to them, but rather they would welcome you; for there is something gracious in your appearance. But if you will, stay here, and we will go home and tell our mother, the lady Metaneira, all your story, so that you may come to our house rather than any other. She nurses in the hall her infant son, late-born, long prayed for, and welcome; and if you brought him up to the age of young manhood, our mother would hasten to reward you in gratitude."

The goddess agreed, and the maidens hurried home with their pitchers. When they found their mother and told her what had passed, she told them to bring the stranger back with them with all the speed they could. Catching up the folds of their garments, they hastened back to the goddess as she waited by the roadside, and led her back to their father's house. They hastened ahead like young deer in the springtime, while Demeter in the grief of her heart walked behind, with her head veiled, draped in the dark-blue cloak that floated around her slender feet.

Soon they came to the house of the just Celeus, and passed through the gateway to where the stately Metaneira sat, leaning against a pillar, with her little son in her arms. As the goddess passed through the entrance, she seemed taller than before, and a divine light glowed around her. Metaneira greeted her with reverence and kindness; but for all that she could do, Demeter would neither sit in a comfortable place nor take food or drink nor smile, so great was her grief.

At Metaneira's request, Demeter undertook to nurse her young son Demophoön, and the child throve under her care, growing like one of the gods. By day Demeter gave him ambrosia, the food of the gods, and at night, when all the house was asleep, she would hold him in the heart of the fire to burn away what was mortal from his nature. By her power she would have made him ageless and deathless forever, if Metaneira had not one wakeful night stood at the door of her scented chamber and seen her, and cried out in fear, "Demophoön, my little son, is the stranger woman burying you in the fire?" Demeter in anger snatched the child from the flames and let him fall onto the palace floor, exclaiming to Metaneira, "You mortals are blind to your destiny, whether good or evil, and never see aright what comes upon you. Your folly has undone my work. I would have made your son ageless and deathless forever, and have bestowed eternal honour upon him, but now he cannot escape death and the fate of men. But he shall have honour all his life, because he was the nursling of the goddess Demeter and lay on my knees and slept in my arms."

So saying, she cast off her old age and weakness: beauty spread round her, and sweet fragrance drifted from her robes, and the house was filled with a brightness like lightning. And she went out from the palace.

When she had gone, for a long time Metaneira was unable to speak or move, or even to pick up her son from the floor. But his sisters heard his pitiful wailing, and sprang out of their comfortable beds; they gathered around him as he struggled, and picked him up and caressed him; but they were less skilful than the divine nurse he had lost, and his heart was not comforted.

When Demeter had travelled far from Eleusis, she sat down and continued to grieve for her daughter. It was a very cruel year for all mankind, since Demeter kept the seed hidden in the ground and the oxen ploughed the fields in vain. Fearing that she would destroy the whole race of men, and that the gods on Olympus would be without their customary honours and sacrifices, Zeus sent Iris, the rainbow-goddess who carries messages for the gods, to speak to Demeter where she sat veiled in her dark-blue cloak in one of her temples.

"Demeter, Father Zeus the all-wise calls you to come back to the councils of the eternal gods; come with me, then, and do not disregard his message."

So said Iris; but her words did not soften the heart of Demeter. Zeus then sent all the eternal and blessed gods to persuade her, offering her gifts and anything else she might wish. But she was still so angry that she swore she would never set foot in Olympus nor let the crops grow until her own fair daughter was restored to her sight.

And when great Zeus saw that she would not relent, he sent swift-footed Hermes down to the underworld, to win over Hades with soft persuasions and bring back Persephone to the light, so that her mother might see her and give up her anger. Hermes descended to the underworld, where he found Hades in his house seated on a couch, with his sad bride beside him. Approaching, he addressed the dark-haired ruler: "King Hades, lord of the dead, Zeus has commanded me to bring the lovely Persephone up to the realm of the gods, so that her mother may see her and cease to be angry with the immortal gods. For now she sits in her temple apart from the gods, brooding a plan to keep the seed hidden forever in the earth, and so to destroy the feeble tribes of men and the honours of the deathless gods."

So he spoke. And Hades, lord of the dead, smiled a grim smile and obeyed the command of Zeus, urging Persephone to return with the messenger. But when she joyfully sprang up to prepare for her return, he took her aside and secretly gave her to eat the seeds of the sweet pomegranate, so that she might not remain forever with her lady mother. Then he harnessed his immortal horses to the golden chariot, and she mounted, and strong Hermes took the reins and whip in his hands and drove swiftly upwards from the dark realm of Hades. And they travelled over land and sea, stopping for nothing until they came to the place where Demeter brooded in her temple.

When Demeter saw them she hastened out to meet them, while Persephone leaped from the chariot and ran and embraced her. But while Demeter still held her dear daughter in her arms, suddenly she began to fear some deception, and she stopped caressing her and asked, "Tell me, my child, surely you did not taste food while you were in the underworld? For if you did not, you can leave the hateful king of the dead forever and live with me and your father, Zeus of the dark clouds; but if you have tasted food, you must go back again to the secret places of the earth for a third part of every year."

Then Persephone wept, and told how she had been persuaded to eat of the pomegranate before her long journey to the upper world. And having taken food in the country of the dead, she could not leave it altogether and be with her mother and honoured by the immortal gods. But Demeter promised her, "Yet when the earth shall blossom with all the flowers of spring, you shall come up from the land of gloom and darkness to gladden the sight of gods and mortal men."

So Persephone was restored to her mother, and Demeter's sorrow was healed and her anger left her; soon the bare fields and plains waved with long ears of corn, and the rich land was busy with preparations for harvest. But for a third part

of every year, Persephone descends to the grave country of
Hades, returning in the spring to gladden gods and men.

ADONIS

> *... Beds of hyacinth and roses*
> *Where young Adonis oft reposes*
> *Waxing well of his deep wound*
> *In slumber soft, and on the ground*
> *Sadly sits the Assyrian queen.*
>
> MILTON

Another young person whose coming is said to bring with it
the fruitfulness of the earth, though this time a mortal, is the
beautiful Adonis, born from a myrrh-tree in Sabaea, the land
of spices. His mother Myrrha was turned into a tree after
offending Aphrodite, the laughter-loving sea-born goddess,
and the drops of precious gum that flow from its bark are the
tears she still sheds for her fault.

When he was still a very young man, Adonis' beauty struck
the heart of Aphrodite, who used to accompany him on the
hunting expeditions in which he delighted. But on one sad
day, when she had just left him in her swan-drawn chariot, a
wild boar rushed out of a thicket and gored Adonis in the
thigh. The boar is said to have been sent by the war-god Ares,
jealous of Aphrodite's attentions to the young huntsman, or to
have been Ares himself in disguise. Adonis sank to the ground,
blood pouring from his wound, and Aphrodite, who heard
from far off his cries of pain and astonishment, arrived only
in time to take him in her arms and see him die. Overcome
with grief, she leaned over his body and washed away the
blood; and as it touched the ground, from every drop there
sprang a flower the colour of blood. Beautiful and frail, its
petals are loosened by the wind that stirs it and from which it

takes its name: wind-flower, anemone.

But there are some who say that Adonis returns every year from the dwelling of the dark queen Persephone, and every year he is slain by the rough boar his enemy and mourned by the great goddess who loves him, while the river Adonis in Lebanon runs red with his blood. In the country festivals held in his honour, baskets of flowers were thrown into the rivers and springs to commemorate his short life, and the mourners would say, "Farewell, dear Adonis, and may you find us all happy when you come again another year."

HYACINTHUS

> *For so Apollo, with unweeting hand,*
> *Whilom did slay his dearly-lovèd mate,*
> *Young Hyacinth, born on Eurotas' strand,*
> *Young Hyacinth, the pride of Spartan land;*
> *But then transformed him to a purple flower.*
>
> MILTON

The Spartan Hyacinthus, the friend of Apollo, also had a life that was pleasant but short. For his sake the god left his oracle and temple at Delphi, and they spent their time together in sports in the open air. Once when they were tired from hunting, they took to throwing the discus in turn to see who could throw it farther; and then it was that Apollo with an unlucky cast struck his companion on the forehead. All Apollo's famous skill in healing was in vain, and Hyacinthus died from the injury. Since he could do nothing to save his friend, Apollo found a way of keeping his memory alive: from Hyacinthus' blood sprang the hyacinth flower, lily-shaped, purple-hued, and marked on its leaves with the Greek letters αιαι, the syllables of grief.

NARCISSUS

Foolish Narcisse, that likes the wat'ry shore.
SPENSER

As beautiful as Adonis was the ill-fated Narcissus, who from
his childhood was loved by all who saw him but whose pride
would let him love no one in return. At last one of those who
had hopelessly courted him turned and cursed him, exclaiming:
"May he suffer as we have suffered! May he too love in vain!"
The avenging goddess Nemesis heard and approved this
prayer.

There was nearby a clear pool, with shining silvery waters.
No shepherd had ever come there, nor beast nor bird nor
falling branch marred its surface: the grass grew fresh and
green around it, and the sheltering woods kept it always cool
from the midday sun.

Here once came Narcissus, heated and tired from the chase,
and lay down by the pool to drink. As he bent over the water,
his eyes met the eyes of another young man, gazing up at
him from the depths of the pool. Deluded by his reflection,
Narcissus fell in love with the beauty that was his own.
Without thought of food or rest he lay beside the pool
addressing cries and pleas to the image, whose lips moved as
he spoke but whose reply he could never catch. Echo came
by, the most constant of his disdained lovers. She was a
nymph who had once angered Hera, the wife of Zeus, by
talking too much, and in consequence was deprived of the use
of her tongue for ordinary conversation: all she could do was
repeat the last words of others. Seeing Narcissus lying there,
she pleaded with him in his own words. "I will die unless you
pity me," cried Narcissus to his beloved. "Pity me," cried
Echo as vainly to hers. Narcissus never raised his eyes to her
at all, though she remained day after day beside him on the

bank, pleading as well as she was able. At last she pined away, withering and wasting with unrequited love, till nothing was left of her but her voice, which the traveller still hears calling unexpectedly in woods and waste places.

As for the cruel Narcissus, he fared no better. The face that looked back at him from the water became pale, thin and haggard, till at last poor Echo caught and repeated his last "Farewell!" But when she came with the other nymphs to lament over his body, it was nowhere to be found. Instead, over the pool bent a new flower, white with a yellow centre, which they called by his name. From this flower the Furies, the avengers of guilt, twist garlands to bind their hateful brows.

ORPHEUS

Orpheus with his lute made trees
And the mountain tops that freeze
Bow themselves when he did sing;
To his music plants and flowers
Ever sprung; as sun and showers
There had made a lasting Spring.

Everything that heard him play,
Even the billows of the sea,
Hung their heads, and then lay by.
In sweet music is such art,
Killing care, and griefs of heart,
Fall asleep, or hearing die.

SHAKESPEARE

Orpheus the Thracian is the magical musician and divine poet of Greek story. Shortly after his marriage to the nymph Eurydice, the young bride while wandering through the meadows was fatally bitten by a snake that had been lurking among the flowers. The grieving Orpheus resolved to take the terrible journey to the underworld in search of her. Singing of his loss to the music of his lyre, he passed Cerberus, the three-headed hell-hound who guards the gate of Hades' sad realm, crossed the river Styx in the boat of Charon, the ferryman of the dead, and stood at last in the grim presence of Hades and Persephone, the only man in all that vast court with breath in his body. So irresistibly touching was his song of lost love that the thin shades wept in sympathy and the torments of the great sufferers, Ixion stretched on his wheel and Sisyphus straining against his rock, for a few moments ceased. Hades himself, the dark king of shades, relented, and told Orpheus that Eurydice might follow him back to the upper world, on one condition: he must not turn back to look at her before they had both reached the light.

Orpheus rejoiced as he began the long journey back, trusting that his wife was behind him. Just as he was approaching the borders of the light, his trust in Hades failed, and in an instant of doubt he turned his head: he saw Eurydice, but instantly her form began to fade. As he embraced her the shades of night pressed round her again and she was gone, leaving him to clasp the empty air.

At this second loss, Orpheus was plunged into grief even more overwhelming. In vain he tried a second time to cross the river of death, pleading to be taken with the waiting shades: the ferryman turned his back. At last he went home to Thrace, where he wandered about the wintry mountains, singing of the happy past and the desolated present. At his sad music the animals forgot to prey on one another and lay peaceably side by side as never since the Golden Age, and trees and stubborn rocks were moved by his song.

Once as he was singing to this audience, a group of Maenads, frenzied women who worshipped the god Dionysus, came by in a wild dance. Seeing the musician, they called out to him to play something cheerful for their revels. When he paid no attention to them but continued his sad strains, they became enraged and fell on him as an enemy of their god, and finally tore him to pieces. His limbs were scattered about the countryside; his head was thrown into the nearby Hebrus river flowing down from the mountains, and as it was borne towards the sea it never ceased to sing. At last the head came ashore at the island of Lesbos, and with it came the gift of song that was to make the island famous for its poets, Arion, Sappho and Alcaeus. Apollo in pity set up a shrine for the head in a grove where the nightingales ever afterwards have sung more beautifully than anywhere else in the world. Some say that when the head was brought ashore it became silent; others, that the sweet voice of Orpheus can still be heard there, uttering oracles and stories of the gods.

Boar

III

LOVES OF THE GODS
AND METAMORPHOSES

LOVES OF ZEUS: CALLISTO, IO

> *The gods themselves,*
> *Humbling their deities to love, have taken*
> *The shapes of beasts upon them: Jupiter*
> *Became a bull, and bellow'd; the green Neptune*
> *A ram, and bleated; and the fire-rob'd god,*
> *Golden Apollo, a poor humble swain.*
>
> SHAKESPEARE

APPARENTLY in the earliest times the forms of things were more fluid than they are now, seeing that the Greeks have many tales of shape-shifting, or metamorphosis, most of them in connection with the love-affairs of the gods.

The god who most regularly fell in love with mortal women was Father Zeus himself. He courted Europa in the form of a bull, Danaë in a shower of gold, and the virtuous Alcmena in the shape of her husband. Leda, whom he visited as a swan, became the mother of two girls, Clytemnestra and Helen, who was said to have been hatched from an egg, and also of the Heavenly Twins, Castor and Polydeuces.

The main hindrance to Zeus' activities was the jealousy of his wife Hera, who did her best to punish him and his conquests.

One of them, Callisto, whom Zeus lured away from hunting with Artemis and her band of nymphs, Hera turned into a bear. After Callisto's son Arcas had grown up and become a huntsman himself, Hera brought him to his mother's den. But as he fitted an arrow to his bow, Zeus carried Callisto up to heaven, where she shines as the Great Bear, later joined by the star Arcturus, her son. In a fury Hera made Poseidon refuse to admit them to his waters, so that they alone of all the constellations never dip below the horizon.

Another unfortunate maiden loved by Zeus was Io, daughter of the river Inachus. When one day Hera saw that the earth was shrouded in clouds and dense darkness, she suspected her wandering husband; and piercing through the clouds, she found him standing beside a fine white cow, into which he had quickly transformed his beloved. Hera pretended to be struck with the cow's beauty, and asked Zeus to give it to her as a present, and for fear of worse he dared not refuse. She immediately gave poor Io into the keeping of Argus, the hundred-eyed watchman, who spied on her day and night, never closing all his eyes at once.

Zeus called his son Hermes, and commanded him to kill Argus. Adopting the disguise of a herdsman, the messenger-god came down to the mountain-top where Argus sat, and began to charm him with stories and with tunes played on a pipe of reeds. Argus became drowsy, and at length closed every one of his hundred eyes: then Hermes sprang up and struck off his head with a single sword-blow.

Hera took the eyes of her faithful servant and placed them in the tail of her own bird, the peacock. She continued her persecution of Io, tormenting her with a gadfly that drove her all over the known world. At length when Io reached the stream of Nile, Hera relented and allowed her to return to her proper form. The Egyptians built temples to her and worshipped her as a goddess.

Maiden with deer

PAN AND SYRINX

> *Pan's Syrinx was a girl indeed,*
> *Though now she's turned into a reed;*
> *From that dear reed Pan's pipe doth come,*
> *A pipe that strikes Apollo dumb;*
> *Nor flute, nor lute, nor gittern can*
> *So chant it as the pipe of Pan.*

> JOHN LYLY

The reed-pipes with which Hermes lulled Argus to sleep have a story of their own. Syrinx, an Arcadian nymph who like Callisto used to hunt on the mountains in Artemis' train, attracted the attention of the goat-footed forest-god Pan, who pursued her over hill and over dale till she reached the shallow river Ladon. Here she stopped and prayed to the nymphs of the stream to help her; and when Pan thought he had caught her, he found himself grasping a handful of marsh reeds. As he stood there sighing, the wind blew through the reeds and drew from them a thin, melancholy music. This almost consoled Pan for the loss of Syrinx: he took reeds of different lengths and fastened them together with wax, producing the first reed-pipes, or Pan-pipes as they are still called after him.

APOLLO AND DAPHNE

> *The gods, that mortal beauty chase,*
> *Still in a tree did end their race:*
> *Apollo hunted Daphne so,*
> *Only that she might laurel grow;*
> *And Pan did after Syrinx speed,*
> *Not as a nymph, but for a reed.*

> MARVELL

A similar story is told of Apollo and Daphne, daughter of the river Peneus. Apollo was incautious enough one day to tease the boy Eros for being a child and carrying toy weapons: Eros thereupon drew two arrows from his quiver and fitted them to his bow. The first, gold-tipped and sharp, flew straight to the heart of Apollo, kindling there the flames of raging love. The other, blunt and leaden, pierced Daphne, making her hate and fear the very name of love. When the two met, in spite of all that Apollo could say she turned and fled from him. Coming in her flight to her father's river, she begged him to take away the beauty that was so troublesome to her; and at once she became a shining, trembling tree. Since the maiden had escaped him, Apollo swore henceforward to love and honour the laurel, which ever afterwards crowned his head and is the token of poet's or conqueror's fame.

CLYTIE

The heart that has truly loved never forgets,
But as truly loves on to the close;
As the sunflower turns on her god when he sets
The same look that she turned when he rose.

THOMAS MOORE

A maiden who loved a god without return was Clytie, whose affections were fixed on the sun-god Helios. Day after day she stood still and gazed at him in his passage across the sky, turning her face to catch the last glimpse as he dropped below the horizon. At last she became fixed in her place, where she now stands as a sunflower, rooted in the ground but still straining to watch the disdainful beloved.

ENDYMION

> *Peace, ho! the moon sleeps with Endymion,*
> *And would not be awak'd.*
>
> SHAKESPEARE

Not only gods but also goddesses were sometimes attracted to mortals. One such was the moon-goddess Selene, who fell in love with the shepherd Endymion as he tended his flocks on Mount Latmos in Caria; she cast him into an eternal sleep so that she could visit him when she liked, and when the night sky is dark, it is because she has descended to the cave where her shepherd sleeps.

ARACHNE

> *The most fine-fingered workwoman on ground,*
> *Arachne.*
>
> SPENSER

The spider was once a young woman, Arachne, who presumptuously challenged Athene to a contest in weaving. The goddess sat down at the loom and very quickly produced a tapestry that showed the rivalry between herself and Poseidon for the guardianship of Athens, not yet bearing her name. Poseidon struck the rocks with his trident, and out sprang a horse, his gift to the people of Attica; but Athene gave them the olive-tree, with its fruit and rich oil and finely-grained hard wood, which was adjudged the better gift. In the corners around this scene, the divine artist worked four little pictures of punishments sent by the gods upon presumptuous mortals.

Arachne, unabashed at the goddess' success, worked on her web pictures of the gods in the various disguises they had worn to deceive mortal women: Zeus as a bull, as a swan and as a shower of gold, Apollo and Poseidon and the others in various unworthy shapes. Athene was angered both by the brilliance of the weaving and by the insult to the gods. Tearing Arachne's tapestry to pieces, she beat her about the head with her shuttle. Arachne in shame tried to hang herself; but Athene immediately transformed her as she dangled from the rope, with the curse that she should not die but remain suspended in the air for all time, both herself and her descendants, shrivelled and eight-legged and eternally spinning thread from her belly.

PROCNE AND PHILOMELA

> *Ah! thought I, thou mourn'st in vain,*
> *None takes pity on thy pain:*
> *Senseless trees they cannot hear thee,*
> *Ruthless beasts they will not cheer thee.*
> *King Pandion he is dead,*
> *All thy friends are lapp'd in lead,*
> *All thy fellow birds do sing*
> *Careless of thy sorrowing.*
> *Even so, poor bird, like thee,*
> *None alive will pity me.*
>
> RICHARD BARNEFIELD

King Pandion of Athens had two daughters, named Procne and Philomela. Procne, the elder, was married to King Tereus of Thrace, and after five years of marriage she asked her husband to let her sister come to visit her. Tereus, agreeing, himself set out by sea to fetch her. But when the lovely Philomela had come aboard the ship, Tereus conceived a wicked passion for her, and instead of taking her to her sister, he landed on the rocky coast and dragged her deep into the

Dionysus

forest, where he kept her in an ancient tower as his captive. So that she should not tell her story, the barbarous king cut out her tongue. Then he returned to the Thracian court, where he told Procne that her sister had died on the journey.

For a whole year Philomela grieved in the dark forest. Then, setting up a rough loom, she wove on it a tapestry in which her story was shown, and by signs instructed a servant to take it to the Thracian queen. Unrolling the tapestry, Procne read the dreadful tale. At once she hastened to the forest, released her sister, and brought her secretly back to the palace, where the two plotted revenge. Seizing Procne's little son, they killed him and cut up his body, cooking the meat in a dish which Procne set before her husband. Not until he had eaten did she tell him what was in it, while Philomela, still dabbled in the child's blood, came out and stood before him. When he understood all, Tereus grasped his sword and pursued the sisters. To prevent more bloodshed the gods at once transformed all three of them: Tereus to a hoopoe wearing a crest of feathers and Procne to a chattering home-dwelling swallow, while Philomela, her voice at last restored, became the nightingale who tells her sorrows all night to the silent woods.

MIDAS' TOUCH

> *Thou gaudy gold,*
> *Hard food for Midas, I will none of thee.*
>
> SHAKESPEARE

Another story of transformation concerns the wine-god Dionysus, whose fat drunken old tutor Silenus one day fell asleep in the garden of King Midas of Phrygia, where he was found by the servants and brought into the palace. Midas recognized Silenus and made much of him, feasting him merrily for ten days, after which Dionysus came to fetch his friend away. In gratitude to Midas, he promised him whatever gift he should ask as a reward, and Midas hastily demanded: "Grant that whatever I touch shall be turned into gold." The god would rather have given him something better, but Midas had made his choice; so he left him to find out about it.

At first Midas was delighted with his boon, touching twigs and stones and flowers and seeing them turn to the finest gold in his hands; but when he sat down to eat and his food and wine became solid metal the moment they touched his mouth, he began to complain bitterly and to implore Dionysus to take back the cruel gift. Seeing him repent of his rashness, Dionysus told him to wash in the nearby river Pactolus: the river took the touch from him, and ever afterwards has had golden sands.

Midas' thoughtlessness was to bring him trouble again. He was once present at a contest in music between the rustic god Pan with his pipes and Apollo with the lyre, when the judge, the wise old mountain Tmolus, decided in favour of the leader of the Muses. Immediately Midas cried out that the decision was unjust and Pan's music the sweeter. The insulted Apollo forced Midas to bear the sign of his foolish judgement, turning his ears to the long grey twitchers of an ass.

Midas, ashamed of this stigma, tried to conceal it by keeping his head wrapped in a purple turban, which only his barber was ever allowed to disturb. Afraid to tell the king's secret and yet longing to share it, the man one day dug a hole in the earth into which he murmured what he had seen, and went his way with a quiet mind. But some reeds grew up out of the earth he had filled in, and they began to whisper among themselves, and when the south wind blew they spoke so that all could hear them: "King Midas has ass's ears."

CEYX AND ALCYONE

The winds with wonder whist
Smoothly the waters kissed,
Whispering new joys to the mild Ocean,
Who now hath quite forgot to rave,
While birds of calm sit brooding on the charmèd wave.

MILTON

The Thessalian king Ceyx once parted from his wife Alcyone, a daughter of Aeolus, to go on a long voyage by sea. The first night after he left her, a storm blew up and wrecked his ship, so that he and all his men were drowned. Meanwhile Alcyone waited at home, without news of her husband, and constantly offered to the gods prayers for his safe return, above all to Hera, the protectress of married love. Wearied with prayers for one already dead, Hera sent Iris to the drowsy house of Sleep, to ask the god to let Alcyone know the truth in a dream. The home of Sleep is a cave where the sun never enters, in a dark and silent countryside. Poppies grow in abundance before the doors, and from the cave flows the slumbrous murmuring river of forgetfulness. Within on a high dark couch lies the god sleeping, and here Iris spoke her message.

From among his many sons Sleep sent Morpheus, the dream-god, to stand at Alcyone's bed-side in the form of her drowned husband, naked and streaming with water. "My poor wife," he said, "do you not know your husband, or has death changed my face? Your prayers did not save me from shipwreck and drowning. Rise up, put on mourning garments, carry out the rites for the dead lest I should descend unwept to the land of shades."

As the figure slipped away, the force of Alcyone's grief woke her, and she hastened down to the shore, where the waves rolled in the body of Ceyx to her feet. Flinging herself in distraction into the water, she was changed by the pitying gods into a kingfisher, and her husband with her. Now every winter for seven calm days Alcyone broods upon the sea, with wings outstretched to cover her floating nest, while her father Aeolus keeps the winds locked up until the little birds are hatched. This period we call the halcyon days.

NISUS AND SCYLLA

> *Ah cease, rash youth! desist ere 'tis too late,*
> *Fear the just gods, and think of Scylla's fate!*
> *Chang'd to a bird, and sent to flit in air,*
> *She dearly pays for Nisus' injur'd hair!*
>
> POPE

The city of Megara on the Isthmus of Corinth was ruled by King Nisus, who among his white hairs had a single purple lock, on which the city's fortune depended. The powerful King Minos of Crete once besieged Megara, and Nisus' daughter Scylla, watching the struggle from a tower in the city wall, soon got to know all the warriors by sight. Among them she was most struck by Minos himself: in fact, she fell violently in love with him and would shortly have done anything to win his favour. She stole one night to her father's bedroom and, as he slept, cut off the charmed lock; then she made her way through the ranks of the enemy to Minos' tent, carrying the lock in her hand. When she came before Minos, she offered it to him as a pledge of her love.

Minos, horrified by Scylla's betrayal of her father, shrank away from the gift and sent her with scorn back to the city. Soon, its ruler's luck being gone, Megara fell into Minos' hands. The Cretans plundered it freely and then set sail for home. Scylla fled down the beach after Minos and seized the rudder of his ship; but she was beaten back by a huge sea-eagle – her father, transformed by the gods. Just as she fell into the water, she too was changed into a sea-bird: the *ciris*, or "shearer", called after her act. And wherever she is seen there too is the sea-eagle, pursuing her with his cries.

PHILEMON AND BAUCIS

> *I saw myself the garlands on their boughs,*
> *And tablets hung for gifts of granted vows;*
> *And offering fresher up, with pious prayer,*
> *The good, said I, are God's peculiar care,*
> *And such as honour heaven, shall heavenly honour share.*
> OVID, TRANSLATED BY DRYDEN

In the countryside of Phrygia an oak and a linden-tree stood side by side, always hung with fresh garlands by those who lived near by. Round about lay a stagnant, marshy lake, the haunt of croaking birds. Once, it is said, Zeus and Hermes, disguised as ordinary travellers, came down to this spot of earth and wandered from house to house seeking hospitality. Everywhere they were refused and turned away, at great houses and small, until Zeus, the special protector of travellers far from home, began to get angry. At last they came to a little cottage, poorly thatched with reeds, whose owners opened the door to them and made them warmly welcome. The old couple, Philemon and his wife Baucis, hastened to offer such comforts as they had. Philemon drew up rickety chairs and invited them to rest themselves, while Baucis put the stew-pot on the fire, feeding the flames with twigs and chips of bark. Bustling about, she soon had a meal spread for the gods – cottagers' fare, smoked bacon cut down from the rafters, vegetables out of the garden, eggs baked among the ashes, served on clay and wooden dishes with a little sour wine. Nuts and fruit, figs, plums, apples and grapes, made up the dessert, with honeycomb besides.

Busy caring for their guests, the old couple did not at first notice that however many times they filled the cups with wine, the pitcher remained full. When this sign of the gods' presence struck them, Baucis and Philemon were alarmed. They begged forgiveness for the humble meal, offering to kill their single goose if only they could catch it. This the gods would not permit. Revealing themselves, they declared that the neighbourhood would be punished for its meanness towards strangers, Philemon and Baucis only excepted. These they invited to come with them to the top of a hill overlooking the district.

When Philemon and Baucis turned on the hill-top to look down, they saw the whole countryside drowned in marshy waters, their cottage alone left standing. As they watched, grieving for the fate of their neighbours, the cottage was changed into a temple, gold-roofed and gleaming with white marble. Then Zeus asked the old man and his wife what gift they would like from him. After a moment's consultation they replied, "To be your priests while we live, and to die at the same instant so that neither of us outlives the other."

Zeus established them in the temple, which they tended for several years. Then when Baucis and Philemon had grown very old, one day as they were reminiscing about the events that had brought them there, each saw the other begin to put forth leaves. "Goodbye, dear friend!" they cried out together. As they spoke, bark closed over their bodies and they were changed into an oak and a linden. The trees were long honoured for the sake of Baucis and Philemon, and as a memorial of the acts of the gods.

IV. THE HEROES

PERSEUS

Danaë in a brazen tower
Where no love was, loved a shower.
                    JOHN FLETCHER

"YOU will have no sons of your own, and your daughter's son will be your death." So ran the answer of the oracle to King Acrisius of Argos, who had come to ask about his future. Acrisius went home in a fury, and promptly shut up his beautiful daughter Danaë in a tower of bronze where no man could see her, but all to no purpose; for Zeus poured himself in at an opening in the roof as a shower of gold, and gave her a son, whom she called Perseus. Resisting the will of the gods, but still reluctant to kill his own flesh and blood, Acrisius set Danaë and her child afloat in a wooden chest, expecting that the raging sea would soon finish them off. But their ark at

Illustration: Gorgon shield

55

length was carried to the island of Seriphos, where a fisherman named Dictys cast his net around it and drew it ashore.

Welcomed by the fisherman and his wife, Danaë and Perseus lived with them for several years. Dictys' brother Polydectes, as harsh as Dictys was kind, was king of the island, and he in time demanded the stranger woman in marriage. He was greatly astonished when Danaë and her son, now fully grown, resisted him, and he resolved that Perseus should be got rid of forthwith. To this end, he gave out that he had decided instead to marry a neighbouring princess and invited the young men of the island, Perseus among them, to a celebration. Each of the guests brought a present: only Perseus in his poverty had none. Taunted for it by Polydectes, he flung back proudly that he was prepared to go out and win by his own efforts a rarer gift than any –"even the head of the Gorgon Medusa herself". That was just what Polydectes had hoped to hear. "Very well," he said, "we will see no more of you till you have it."

> *What was that snaky-headed Gorgon shield*
> *That wise Minerva wore, unconquered virgin,*
> *Wherewith she freezed her foes to congealed stone?*
>
> MILTON

The original Gorgons were two monstrous sisters, bird-winged, snake-haired, and plain-faced enough to scare off anything, living on a solitary rock at the edge of the western sea. These two were divinely born and immortal, but a mortal woman had been sent to join them as punishment for a crime against the gods. She, Medusa, was the most terrible of the three, with a face so appalling in its ugliness and hatred that whoever looked at it was turned into stone.

Perseus' task would have been impossible had he not been helped by Pallas Athene and by Hermes, the messenger of the gods. Giving him a brightly-polished shield of bronze, Athene

warned him never to look directly at the face of the Gorgon
but only at its reflection in the mirror-like surface. Hermes
lent him his own winged sandals to shorten the long journey
and a sickle of adamant with which to cut off the Gorgon's
head. They both gave him advice about the beings he must
seek out for the remaining information and equipment he
needed.

The first place to which Perseus' winged sandals carried him
was the home of the Gorgons' three sisters, the white-haired
Graeae, dwelling in the farthest west. These had only one eye
and one tooth among them, and Perseus easily got control
over them by snatching the eye as they were passing it from
hand to hand, and threatening to throw it into the sea. They
were quickly persuaded to direct him to the Gorgons' rock
and to give him the things he asked for: a helmet of invisibility
to wear when he was about to strike, and a leather wallet in
which the head could safely be carried.

Arriving at the Gorgons' rock, he found the three horrors
asleep. This gave him time to decide which was Medusa, the
only one who could be killed: to attack either of the others
would have been fatal. Hovering over her in his winged
sandals, he struck off her head with one blow and dropped it
into the leather wallet. The sister Gorgons woke at the noise
and howled in fury at the murder, but Perseus sprang into the
air, concealed by the helmet of darkness. As he flew back
towards the east, drops of the Gorgon's blood fell from the
wallet onto the Libyan sands, where they became all manner
of snakes: that is why to this day the Sahara desert swarms
with deadly serpents.

> . . . *that starred Ethiop queen that strove*
> *To set her beauty's praise above*
> *The Sea-Nymphs, and their powers offended.*
> MILTON

On his way back to the court of Polydectes, Perseus met with another adventure. He was flying over the land of Ethiopia when he saw a maiden on the seashore, chained to a rock, her arms outstretched against it. Hastening down, he learned her story from her. She was the unfortunate Andromeda, whose mother Queen Cassiopeia, glorying in her beauty, had boasted that she excelled all the daughters of the sea-god Nereus. To avenge the insult, Nereus had sent a sea-monster, whose ravages of crops and men could be checked only by the sacrifice of the princess. While they were still speaking, the monster appeared out to sea, swimming towards the shore. Perseus, standing in front of Andromeda, snatched the head from its pouch and held it aloft, making his first trial of its powers. Instantly the great serpent stopped; its coils congealed; it was no longer a living creature, but an immense black rock, stretching far out into the waves. Before putting the head away again, Perseus laid it for a moment on some seaweed, which stiffened and became the first coral.

Andromeda's grateful parents gave her to Perseus in marriage, and she accompanied him on his return to Seriphos. They found on arrival that far from marrying a princess from the mainland, as he had said he meant to do, Polydectes was still pursuing Danaë with his attentions, and that she and her protector Dictys had taken refuge in a nearby temple. Perseus went straight to the palace, where the king and his nobles were banqueting just as they were when he saw them last. "Here is the promised gift, O King"; and with that he showed them all the head. Visitors to the island are still shown the circle of stones he left behind him. Then, having no more use for the Gorgon's head, Perseus gave it to his protectress Athene, who attached it to the shield that she carries in battle.

Leaving the kingdom to Dictys, Perseus with his wife and his mother crossed the sea to Argos, hoping that Acrisius would by now have forgotten his fears and be prepared to receive them. Far from it: Acrisius fled to a neighbouring kingdom. Perseus, unaware of this, happened to come there shortly afterwards to compete in the funeral games held for the king's old father. When Perseus threw the discus, the wind carried it aside so that it struck Acrisius as he stood in the crowd and killed him. Perseus buried his grandfather with due honour, recognizing in the accident the will of the gods, and returned to inherit the kingdom of Argos. There he and his family lived long and happily, and to him was born a son whose child in turn was Alcmena, the mother of Heracles, the greatest of the heroes of Greece.

THE LABOURS OF HERACLES

> *Great Hercules is presented by this imp,*
> *Whose club kill'd Cerberus, that three-headed* canis;
> *And when he was a babe, a child, a shrimp,*
> *Thus did he strangle serpents in his* manus.
>
> **SHAKESPEARE**

Of all the heroes of the Greeks, Heracles was the strongest and the bravest. He and his twin brother Iphicles, a very ordinary person, were born at Thebes to a mortal woman, Alcmena, after Zeus visited her disguised as her husband. Zeus intended his son to be a great king, but he reckoned without the jealousy of Hera, who was enraged at his unfaithfulness. On the day when Heracles was supposed to be born, Hera heard Zeus declare: "He that is born today of my blood shall rule over all his neighbours." She immediately hastened to Thebes and sat down by the door of Alcmena's room, cross-legged and with her arms and fingers crossed. Not only did she design thus to hinder the birth, she also prevented Eileithyia the birth-goddess from entering the room for seven days and seven nights. On the first day a boy of Zeus' blood was born at Mycenae, Eurystheus, another descendant of Perseus, so that Heracles was robbed of his royal birthright. But the jealous Hera might never have let him be born at all if she had not been tricked in her turn: one of Alcmena's maids, suspecting magic, raised a cry of rejoicing as if her mistress had been delivered, and when Hera in astonishment sprang to her feet, Eileithyia slipped into the room and the twins were born.

Before Alcmena's babies were a year old, Hera sent two serpents into the nursery to kill them. The shrieks of Iphicles brought the whole household running: when they got there, Heracles was laughing in his cradle, a strangled snake drooping in each small fist. From that night it was clear that the child was marked out for a special destiny.

> *Like that great champion of the antique world*
> *Whom famous poets' verse so much doth vaunt*
> *And hath for twelve huge labours high extolled . . .*
>
> SPENSER

When he came to manhood, Heracles earned the gratitude of his fellow-Thebans by driving off a neighbouring king who had long been troubling them, and in reward he was given the hand of the princess, by whom he had three sons. After he had enjoyed several years of happy marriage, Hera sent upon him a fit of madness, in which he killed his wife and children. In his remorse after he returned to his senses, he was not satisfied with the formal rite of purification from blood-guilt, but demanded a suitable penance of Apollo's oracle at Delphi. There the priestess counselled him to seek his kinsman King Eurystheus and serve him for twelve years in whatever way he should command. In the penance set by Eurystheus consist the famous Twelve Labours of Heracles. The oracle said further that at the conclusion of his labours he would become one of the immortals.

The first of Heracles' labours was to kill the Nemean Lion, a huge animal whose skin was proof against all weapons. After trying in vain to subdue it with arrows, sword, and the heavy olive-wood club he always carried, Heracles seized it in his arms and choked it to death. Henceforward he wore its skin round his shoulders as a cloak. His second labour was to kill the Hydra, the serpent offspring of a pair of monsters, that lived in the swamp of Lerna. It had nine heads, each of which sprouted anew if cut off. Heracles dealt with this hazard by cutting off the heads and then cauterizing the stumps before they could grow again. The third, fourth and fifth labours were the killing or capturing of the Erymanthian Boar, the golden-horned Hind of Ceryneia, and the man-eating Stymphalian Birds, which shot their sharp metallic feathers like darts at all who came near them. Sixth, Heracles had to clean out in a single day the stables of King Augeas, where dung had been accumulating year after year: this he did by diverting the course of a river and letting it carry the filth away. The seventh labour was the capture of a wild bull that was laying waste the crops of Crete. The eighth was the capture of four mares that the cruel king Diomedes regularly fed with the flesh of guests visiting the palace: Heracles flung them the body of their master, whereupon they became tame. The ninth labour was the acquisition of the golden girdle belonging to Hippolyta, the queen of the Amazons, which Heracles carried off partly by bravery and partly by charm. The tenth was to fetch the cattle of Geryon, a king with three bodies and three heads who kept his herds on a western island towards the sunset. Heracles sailed there in a golden cup that he borrowed from the Sun, setting up on the way two famous pillars at the far end of the Mediterranean, at the points of rock now called Ceuta and Gibraltar. He then had to kill first Geryon's dog, next his

Heracles in the Cup of the Sun

herdsman, last Geryon himself, before he could load the cattle
into the cup and carry them back to Mycenae.

> *Before thee stands this fair Hesperides*
> *With golden fruit, but dangerous to be touch'd,*
> *For death-like dragons here affright thee hard.*
>
> **SHAKESPEARE**

Heracles' eleventh and twelfth labours were the hardest of
all. First he had to take the steep road down to the underworld
and bring up Cerberus, the three-headed watchdog of the
infernal gate. It was on this expedition that he released his
cousin Theseus from the Chair of Forgetfulness. Last of all,
he was to journey to the western end of the world and bring
back some fruit from the golden apple-tree guarded by the
serpent Ladon and three nymphs called the Hesperides.

Not knowing how to proceed with this task, Heracles set out in search of the wise old sea-god Nereus. Finding him asleep beside the river Po, he seized him and began to ask him what to do. To escape him, Nereus changed his form rapidly into a whole series of creatures, as some sea-gods had the power of doing; but Heracles held him fast until Nereus gave his advice: to persuade the giant Atlas to get the apples for him.

When Heracles reached the Garden of the Hesperides, he saw Atlas standing there, bent under the burden of the sky, and asked him for help. Now Atlas was reluctant to see the garden robbed, as he was its guardian; but an oracle had told him many years before that some day a son of Zeus would come and strip the tree, and moreover, he saw a chance of escaping from his burden. So he agreed to fetch the apples if Heracles would take the weight of the sky for a few minutes; and soon he came back, smiling and tossing the apples from hand to hand. "Hero, you can stand there a little longer, and I'll take these to Eurystheus myself." "Very well, comrade, if you'll just take the sky a minute while I roll my lion-skin into a pad for my shoulders." The foolish Atlas bent under the sky again, and Heracles snatched up the apples and walked off.

> *Earth's son Antaeus . . . in Irassa strove*
> *With Jove's Alcides, and oft foil'd still rose,*
> *Receiving from his mother Earth new strength,*
> *Fresh from his fall, and fiercer grapple join'd,*
> *Throttl'd at length in the air, expir'd and fell.*
>
> MILTON

On his way back to Eurystheus, Heracles met and defeated the Libyan giant Antaeus, who wrestled with all comers and used their skulls to roof a temple he was building. He was the more terrible an opponent because every time he touched the ground his mother Earth renewed his strength, however weary he might be: Heracles overcame him by holding him high in the air until he became as weak as a child and was easily crushed. Before leaving Africa Heracles killed the blood-thirsty Egyptian king Busiris, who used to sacrifice all strangers to Zeus. Making his way to Troy, he arrived just in time to rescue a maiden called Hesione who was about to be sacrificed by her father to a sea-monster. Heracles leapt into the open mouth of the creature and struggled for three days in its belly, slashing about with club and sword until at last it was mortally struck and he cut his way out. It was on this journey too that Heracles travelled to the Caucasus Mountains and released Prometheus from his long sufferings.

Less glorious than these exploits was Heracles' action when in a fit of anger he killed a young man who was a guest under his roof and Zeus, who always upholds the laws of hospitality, decreed as punishment that he must be sold into slavery for a year. The divine messenger Hermes led him into Asia Minor and sold him to Queen Omphale of Lydia, who completed his disgrace by making him sit dressed as a woman among her maiden attendants, turning his clumsy fingers to spinning and weaving, while she draped herself in his lion-skin and played at wielding his club.

> *Methought I saw my late espousèd saint*
> *Brought to me like Alcestis from the grave,*
> *Whom Jove's great son to her glad husband gave,*
> *Rescu'd from death by force though pale and faint.*
>
> MILTON

Besides harrowing the underworld and capturing the apples of immortality, Heracles had another contest with death. When Zeus, as we shall see, struck down the presumptuous healer Asclepius, his father Apollo, not daring to take a direct revenge on the ruler of the gods, murdered the Cyclopes who had made the fatal thunderbolt in their underworld smithy. In punishment Zeus bound Apollo in servitude to a mortal man, King Admetus of Pherae, whose shepherd and herdsman he became. Admetus and his wife Alcestis treated him with great kindness, and in return he obtained from the three Fates (some say by making them drunk) the promise that Admetus' approaching death-day could be postponed if another would consent to die in his place. Admetus went to everyone he could think of, including his old father and mother, imploring them to give up their lives for him: all refused but Alcestis his wife. When the day came, Alcestis quietly died and the household went into mourning for her. At this point Heracles came by on his way to Thrace to tackle the mares of Diomedes, and Admetus thought it right to welcome him without mentioning his cause for sorrow. However, Heracles found out from the servants about Alcestis' sacrifice, and immediately resolved to fight Death himself for her. He lay in wait beside her tomb until the messenger from the underworld appeared, and then challenged him to a wrestling-match, in which the hero was soon the winner. Then taking the restored Alcestis by the hand, he led her to her husband in thanks for the hospitality he had received.

> *The shirt of Nessus is upon me; teach me,*
> *Alcides, thou mine ancestor, thy rage;*
> *Let me lodge Lichas on the horns o' the moon;*
> *And with those hands, that grasp'd the heaviest club,*
> *Subdue my worthiest self.*
>
> **SHAKESPEARE**

After the death of his wife Heracles married a maiden named Deianeira. As he was bringing his bride home, they were stopped by a river in flood. Heracles was able to get over by himself and the centaur Nessus, who was the local ferryman, offered to carry Deianeira. In mid stream he turned and attempted to run off with her, whereupon Heracles shot him with his bow. As Nessus lay dying, he murmured to Deianeira that she should take some of his blood and keep it as a charm: if a time should ever come when Heracles ceased to love her, she could win him back by smearing some of it on a garment for him to wear. Deianeira kept the blood for several years, until she heard a rumour that Heracles was enamoured of a captive princess whom he was bringing home with him from the successful siege of a city. Deianeira sent a messenger to meet him with presents, among them a newly-woven shirt dyed in the blood of Nessus, thus unwittingly bringing to pass the prophecy of an old oracle: "No living man shall be the death of Heracles: by a dead enemy shall he be brought low." Heracles put on the shirt to offer sacrifices to the gods, and immediately he felt his flesh burn in consuming pain. He tried to tear the garment from his back, but the magic substance made it stick fast. Yelling with agony, he seized the unfortunate messenger and flung him into the sea. Then he called aloud to the gods for death; but because of his divine birth, the poison that tormented him could not kill him. To end his suffering, he asked his friends and servants to build him a great pyre on Mount Oeta and place him on it: there among the flames his mortal part was burned away, while his immortal part was carried up to Olympus in the chariot of Zeus. Hera at last relented from her long enmity and married him to her daughter Hebe, the gods' cup-bearer, and in the halls of the gods Heracles enjoys a merry afterlife, feasting and recalling the heroic deeds that raised him above the common fate of men.

Sons of Boreas pursuing the Harpies

JASON AND THE GOLDEN FLEECE

> *Her name is Portia . . . and her sunny locks*
> *Hang on her temples like a golden fleece,*
> *Which makes her seat of Belmont Colchis' strand,*
> *And many Jasons come in quest of her.*
>
> SHAKESPEARE

Aeson, the king of Iolcos in Thessaly, was deposed from his throne by his covetous half-brother Pelias. Fearing for the life of his young son Jason, Aeson brought him to Cheiron, the wise Centaur who lived in a cave in the side of Mount Pelion. Endowed with prodigious strength and nobility, half man, half horse, Cheiron was entrusted with many of the sons of the heroes to be trained in all the heroic arts, as well as the gentler ones of healing and song. When Jason had learned all that Cheiron could teach him, he set out for Iolcos to claim his father's kingdom.

On his way to the seashore city, he had to cross on foot the tumultuous river Anauros, without ferry, bridge or ford. There he met a poor old woman, who begged him to carry her across. This he did with some difficulty, but with no more mishap than the loss of one of his sandals; and when he set her down on the further bank, the old woman revealed herself as the goddess Hera, henceforward his protectress.

When Jason reached Iolcos, he enquired his way to the palace of Pelias and soon stood before the usurper. Pelias trembled to see him, recognizing the man by whom he should be overthrown; for he had long ago been warned by an oracle: "Beware of the man with one sandal." However, he dissembled his fears, and when Jason said who he was and what he had come for, Pelias welcomed him with smooth words. "But, nephew, perhaps you can give me a word of advice. What would you do with a man from whom your life was in danger?" "I would send him to fetch me the Golden Fleece." "Nephew, you are that man."

A generation before Jason's own time, King Athamas of Boeotia married trouble in the form of his second wife, Ino the daughter of Cadmus. Athamas had two children by a former marriage, Phrixus and his sister Helle. Their stepmother Ino hated them, and conceived a plot to get rid of them. One year she secretly roasted the country's entire supply of seed-corn, so that the countrymen, though they sowed as usual, waited in vain for the harvest. When, as Ino expected, her husband sent messengers to enquire of the oracle at Delphi why the land was so afflicted, she bribed them to bring back a false report that the god was angry and demanded the deaths of Phrixus and Helle. Athamas, to save his people from famine, sorrowfully consented to the sacrifice. But just as the priest stood over the children with his knife, Zeus in pity sent a golden ram, that miraculously appeared before the altar. It took the children on its back and fled away with them through the air, over the unknown eastern sea. As they were passing the narrow strait that separates Europe from Asia, Helle slipped from the ram's back and was drowned in the waters that are called after her the Hellespont, or Helle's Sea. Her brother Phrixus hung on until the ram set him down in distant Colchis at the far end of the stormy Euxine Sea. There Phrixus in gratitude sacrificed the ram to Zeus, and its fleece was hung on a tree in a sacred grove and guarded by a dragon. There too in time he married Chalciope, the daughter of Helios' son King Aietes, and there while still quite young he died.

And now, Pelias told Jason, the ghost of his kinsman
Phrixus came to him night after night in dreams, begging him
to recover the fleece and take it back to his old homeland, so
that his troubled spirit might find rest. If Jason could carry
out the task, Pelias would gladly restore to him his father's
kingdom. But in his heart he hoped the young man would
never return.

> *But silent sat the heroes by the oar,*
> *Hearkening the sounds borne from the*
>   *lessening shore;*
> *The lowing of the doomed and*
>   *flower-crowned beasts,*
> *The plaintive singing of the ancient priests,*
> *Mingled with blare of trumpets, and the sound*
> *Of all the many folk that stood around*
> *The altar and the temple by the sea.*
> *So sat they pondering much and silently,*
> *Till all the landward noises died away,*
> *And, midmost now of the green sunny bay,*
> *They heard no sound but washing of the seas*
> *And piping of the following western breeze,*
> *And heavy measured beating of the oars;*
> *So left the Argo the Thessalian shores.*
>
>   WILLIAM MORRIS

The first thing Jason did was to send messengers to all the
cities of Greece to summon the heroes to the quest; and Hera,
his friend, kindled in their hearts the love of glory. One of the
first who came was the shipwright Argus, and to him Jason
entrusted the building of their vessel, the first large ship ever
to put out on the sea, called after her maker the Argo. Fixed
in her bow was a piece of wood from the talking oak of
Dodona, which gave advice when asked, and she had places
for fifty oarsmen. Among the Argonauts, the fifty heroes who

sailed in her, were many of the noblest of Greece: Heracles the strong man with his armour-bearer Hylas, Castor and Polydeuces the twin sons of Zeus, Peleus the father of Achilles, Mopsus the soothsayer who knew the language of the birds, Orpheus the sweet singer, Zetes and Calais the sons of the North Wind, and many more.

The Argo first sailed northwards along the eastern shore of Greece, and then struck east through the Hellespont into the Propontine Sea. At Cius they stopped while Heracles, who had broken his oar, looked for wood for a new one. After uprooting a large fir-tree, which he dragged behind him, Heracles came back to his companions to find that his young armour-bearer was not with them. He began to crash about in the forest, roaring "Hylas! Hylas!" at the top of his great voice. But Hylas was out of hearing. Having set off on his own to look for water, he had come to a deep pool and leaned over it with his pitcher; and the nymph of the spring, seeing the charming boy, caught him by the arms and drew him down to her underwater world. So Heracles never found him again, but wandered the whole night up and down, calling "Hylas! Hylas!" till all the shore resounded. And the Argo sailed on without him.

Their next adventure occurred shortly after they entered the Euxine Sea, in the realm of King Phineus. Phineus was one of the sons of Agenor sent out in search of their sister Europa, carried off by Zeus, and he had come thus far in his wanderings and never returned home. But that was long ago, and now he was an old and wretched man. His one gift, that of prophecy, had proved no blessing to him, for by it he had angered the gods, who sent blindness upon him and moreover plagued him with a pair of Harpies. These were flying monsters with the bodies of women and the wings of hawks, who every time the table was spread before him burst into the palace with a terrible clatter, swooped down on the food, and fled away with it shrieking, spattering dirt on any they left behind. Because they were messengers of the gods' vengeance, they were known as "the hounds of Zeus". No sooner had the poor old king laid a banquet to welcome the heroes, than the loathsome creatures appeared. Immediately Calais and Zetes, the winged sons of Boreas, sprang into the air in pursuit; and some say they are chasing them yet, in the squalls and black airs that vex the Euxine Sea. But the Harpies never troubled King Phineus again; and in return for this service, he gave Jason good advice about the further conduct of his voyage.

One of the dangers about which Phineus warned the Argonauts was the Symplegades, the clashing blue rocks that barred their way, grinding against each other with fearsome noises. Here Jason let loose a dove, which sped only just in time through a narrow passage-way, losing a few tail-feathers as the rocks crashed together behind. As soon as they drew apart again, the Argonauts heaved powerfully on their oars and drove the ship through before the passage could close, as Phineus had told them they must do.

After many long days of rowing eastward along the shore, the heroes sighted the snow-covered Caucasian Mountains that mark the eastern limit of the Euxine Sea. On the highest lay stretched out the Titan Prometheus, with the eagle of vengeful Zeus tearing at his liver: at the foot of the range lay the land of Colchis, the goal of their journey. Entering the mouth of the river Phasis, the Argonauts rowed up it to the grove of Ares and the city of Aietes, child of the Sun, where in a shady backwater they cast anchor and passed the night in consultation.

> *As that brave son of Aeson, which by charms*
> *Achiev'd the golden fleece in Colchid land,*
> *Out of the earth engendered men of arms*
> *Of dragon's teeth, sown in the sacred sand . . .*
>
> **SPENSER**

When dawn broke, Jason with a few chosen comrades set out for the palace of Aietes, built for him by the divine smith Hephaestus. With the king lived his queen, their daughters Chalciope the widow of Phrixus and Medea the witch-maiden, priestess of the dark goddess Hecate, and their young son Absyrtus. Jason came boldly into the presence of Aietes and declared his errand. Now Aietes valued the Golden Fleece as the treasure of his realm, and had no intention of parting lightly with it to any stranger; but he disguised the anger in his heart and proposed to Jason a trial of strength.

"If you are indeed a descendant of the gods and as worthy a man as I myself, then I will give you the Fleece to carry back with you. But first you must prove your merit by accomplishing a prodigious feat, though one within my own powers. Hephaestus made for me two brazen bulls, breathing fire from their jaws: these I yoke on the field of Ares and with them do a full day's ploughing, casting into the furrows teeth from the serpent Cadmus slew. Immediately there springs up a strange harvest of armed men, and as they rise I cut them down into the ploughed earth until none is left. No man who fails to carry out this task as I can shall bear away the Fleece."

When Jason heard this challenge, his courage almost failed him; but now that he had brought his companions so far into foreign lands, he had no choice but to accept. His face was troubled as he turned to go back to the ship. But the goddesses who befriended him, Hera and Athene, shed grace and beauty on him as he walked, so that he shone out from among the crowd. And the heart of Aietes' daughter Medea was stirred in his favour, so that she put away the veil from her face and followed him with her eyes. All night she lay wakeful, troubled with love for Jason and fears for his safety, and then again with shame at her disloyalty to her father who saw this stranger as an enemy.

In the morning Medea's mind was made up. She sent a messenger to ask Jason to meet her at the shrine of Hecate, and then calling her maids she set out for the appointed place. When she met the hero, she was so overcome by her conflicting feelings that she could scarcely speak, and Jason had to strain to catch her words.

"When night comes, go apart from your companions and offer sacrifice to the powerful goddess Hecate, patroness of magic and sorcery: then turn away, and do not let anything you hear, whether the baying of hounds or the trampling of feet, make you look back, if you ever want to return to your companions. At dawn, steep in water this charm I give you and anoint your body all over with it, also your weapons: then for a single day you will be invulnerable, so that neither the breath of the fiery bulls nor the clashing of the earth-born men can harm you. When the dragon's crop springs up, cast among the armed men a great stone, and they will turn against one another and shorten your labour. Then the king will give you the Fleece, and you will sail away to your dear native land; but what will become of me, poor maiden, who have betrayed my father to save a stranger's life?" Moved by her grief, Jason swore to the princess that if with her help he succeeded, she should return with him to Iolcos, where he would marry her. So Medea returned comforted with her maids to her father's palace.

When Jason came back to his companions at the Argo and told them all that had passed, the heroes rejoiced that he had found help against the wicked schemes of Aietes: all but one, who bitterly reproached him. "Son of Aeson, is it now come to this, that we who are men, skilled in the deeds of war, rely on the arts of Aphrodite, on magic, and on the wiles of young girls? Shame, I say, shame and empty folly." But all the others approved Jason's agreement with the fair-haired witch-maiden.

Now night was falling, and Jason took his way to a lonely place, a meadow under the open sky, where he dug a pit, killed a sheep and kindled a fire under it, letting the blood soak into the ground and pouring libations of honey, all the while calling on dark Hecate, goddess of enchantments. And from the depths of the earth the dread goddess heard him, and came herself to the sacrifice offered by Aeson's son; and with her approach serpents twined in the nearby oak boughs, torches shone in the darkness, and about her howled the hounds of hell. Jason saw and heard these things, and felt the ground tremble under him; but he remembered Medea's words, and quickly sought the ship without looking back.

When dawn came, Aietes arrayed himself in his armour, placing on his head a golden helmet that gleamed like the sun as it rises; then mounting his swift-drawn chariot he drove out of the city to the field of Ares, attended by a great multitude of the Colchians. Meanwhile Jason had bathed himself in the water in which he had steeped Medea's charm, and also bathed his weapons; and godlike strength entered into him, and great courage, so that he longed for the contest. The heroes stood around him shouting with joy and hope. When all were assembled, the bulls came charging out from their underground stable, wrapped in black smoke and breathing forth flames of fire, so that all who saw them were afraid. But Jason stood firm before their onset, warding off their sharp horns with his shield, protected from the withering heat by Medea's charm. Then, grasping the horn of one of the bulls, he brought it to its knees, and next the other, and fastened to their necks the adamantine yoke fashioned for King Aietes by Hephaestus, the divine smith. Taking in his hand a bronze helmet filled with the dragon's teeth, he began his day's ploughing of Ares' field, moving steadily along the dark furrows, undaunted by the angry plunging of the bulls.

At evening Jason loosed the bulls from the yoke and drove

them from the field. Already the strange harvest began to cleave the earth, first the gleam of helmets showing above the surface, then whole bodies of fully-armed men springing into view; and each one as he rose turned on Jason as his fated enemy. But Jason quickly threw into their midst a great boulder, and immediately they began to fight among themselves, destroying one another in merciless slaughter, while Jason rushed in and out of the combat dealing fearful blows. The furrows of the field were filled with blood as the last of the earth-born died. And bitterness filled the heart of King Aietes, who turned away from the contest and went back to the city, plotting the destruction of Jason and his comrades.

When Medea heard all that had happened, she felt sure that her father did not mean to honour his promise. Taking her last look at the home of her childhood, she passed out through the gates in the dark, veiling her face and speeding past the watchmen. As she fled, the rising moon caught sight of her and murmured in triumph: "Then I am not the only maiden betrayed by love, when I hasten down the sky to the cave on Mount Latmos where the shepherd Endymion sleeps! Many times you have driven me away and darkened me with your spells, and now you too suffer: for some god has given you Jason to be your grief." But Medea fled on till she came to the shore where the Argo lay at anchor, and called to the sailors to take her aboard.

"Aietes knows all and is plotting some treachery: save yourselves before day breaks and he mounts his chariot in pursuit. And I myself will lull to sleep the fierce dragon and give you the fleece of gold: but, stranger, son of Aeson, swear before the gods the oath you swore to me alone, and now that I have forsaken my country and my friends, do not leave me to shame and dishonour." And Jason swore once more, calling Zeus and Hera to witness, that when they came home to Iolcos he would make her his wife.

Meet I an infant of the house of York,
Into as many gobbets will I cut it
As wild Medea young Absyrtus did.

SHAKESPEARE

Then they rowed the ship up the river to the grove of Ares, and Jason and Medea landed opposite the oak-tree where the Golden Fleece hung, dazzling to the eye and reflecting the beams of the sun just rising. But in front of it stirred the unsleeping dragon, moving his head from side to side and hissing so that the river-bank echoed and mothers still sleeping in the town held their children closer. And Medea stepped up to him, calling on Hecate and on Hypnos the god of sleep to help her, and singing lullabies, so that his cruel head sank to the ground in harmless slumber, and his numberless coils lay spread about the grove. Then Jason snatched the Golden Fleece and held it tightly to him, and he and Medea returned to the Argo, where the heroes had watched the approach of the treasure, gleaming through the trees. And Jason placed Medea in the stern, and the Argonauts shouted and pulled on the oars to carry the ship down to the mouth of the river.

By now Medea's part in aiding the heroes was known to King Aietes and all the people of Colchis, and countless as the leaves that fall in autumn they armed themselves and thronged clamouring along the river-bank, while above them all shone the king in his well-made chariot. But already the Argo, borne on by the swift Phasis and the strength of her oarsmen, had reached the open sea. And the king in anger and grief lifted his hands to Helios his father and Zeus the ruler of the gods to witness the wrongs done against him; and against his own people he uttered threats of vengeance unless they would pursue the strangers and bring back the witch-maiden Medea.

So he spoke; and the whole nation of the Colchians put to sea in pursuit. But the cunning Medea had brought with her the young prince, her brother Absyrtus. And with treacherous hand she struck him down on the decks, so that his blood stained her silver robe as she shrank from his fall; and she cut his body into pieces and threw them overboard to delay the pursuers, who stopped and gathered them aboard the Colchian ships for burial. By this cruel means they were able to outstrip the fleet of Aietes; and cheered by the songs of Orpheus, they sped before a favouring wind along the Euxine Sea.

> *So sung he joyously, nor knew that they*
> *Must wander yet for many an evil day*
> *Or ever the dread Gods should let them come*
> *Back to the white walls of their long-left home.*
>
> WILLIAM MORRIS

The slaying of Absyrtus brought upon the heroes the grievous wrath of Zeus, king of the gods, who stirred up storm-winds to block their way on the sea. And now they must all have perished on the wide sea and never come again to their dear native land; but as they were tossing hither and thither a voice called to them, speaking from the beam of their hollow ship that Athene had set in the prow from the sacred wood of Dodona. And fear seized upon them as it told of the anger of Zeus, declaring that they should not escape alive from the endless roads of the sea and the deadly tempests unless the enchantress Circe purified them from the blood-guilt of Absyrtus' murder. So spoke the ship in the dark night.

And they left the Euxine Sea and passed by the great mainland rivers of the north to the Italian shore and the famous island of Aiaia, the home of bright-haired Circe, child of the Sun. And they found her bathing her head in the salt sea-spray, sorely troubled by visions of the night. For she dreamed that the walls and chambers of her palace ran with blood; and now she was bathing her hair and her garments for a purification. And strange beasts surrounded her, as flocks follow their shepherd, beasts of mixed and uncertain forms. While the heroes gazed in wonder, Jason and Medea followed Circe to her palace. There they refused the seats she offered them, sitting as suppliants in the dust of the hearth, with downcast faces; and Jason fixed in the ground the great sword with which Absyrtus was slain. Then Circe understood her dream, and that they had come to her for purification from guilt of blood. And she offered sacrifice and burned cakes for an atonement, praying that the avenging Furies might relent and Zeus show them favour.

When the rites were done, Circe raised them and seated them, and began to question them concerning their country and their journey; and when Medea raised her eyes, Circe knew her for her kinswoman. For those of the race of Helios are recognized by the gold gleam that flashes from their eyes. So the daughter of sorrowful Aietes told her all she asked, speaking softly in the Colchian tongue, of the quest and the wanderings of the heroes, and the trials set Jason, and her own sin and sorrow in aiding him; but of the murder of Absyrtus she did not tell. Nevertheless the enchantress knew all, and said to her, "Wicked are the ways that you have devised, and shameful shall be your homecoming. But since you have come to me as a suppliant and kinswoman, I shall do you no harm: go on your way with this unknown man you have chosen, the enemy of your kin." And Medea veiled her face and wept, trembling as Jason led her from Circe's halls.

> ... *the Sirens three*
> *Amid'st the flowery-kirtled Naiades*
> *Culling their potent herbs and baleful drugs,*
> *Who as they sung, would take the prisoned soul*
> *And lap it in Elysium. Scylla wept*
> *And chid her barking waves into attention,*
> *And fell Charybdis murmur'd soft applause.*
>
> MILTON

When Hera saw that they were resuming their journey, she called to the rainbow-goddess Iris to seek out Thetis, the silver-footed sea-nymph Zeus had given in marriage to the hero Peleus. Thetis came to her from the chambers of the sea, and Hera said: "The Argonauts, who are under my protection, are about to pass the twin perils, Scylla and Charybdis. Now in the name of our old friendship and the many favours we have done each other, lend your aid to the heroes, among whom is your husband Peleus, so that neither shall Charybdis on one side draw them down into her whirlpool, nor deadly Scylla on the other snatch them up in her horrible jaws." And Thetis consenting set out on the paths of the sea in search of her sisters.

But before the Argo reached Scylla and Charybdis she had to pass the flowering island of the clear-voiced Sirens, whose forms were partly like birds and partly like maidens, who beguiled passing sailors with their sweet songs and lured them ashore to destroy them. There Orpheus took up his lyre, singing and playing so that the songs of the Sirens were quite drowned out. Only one of the heroes still listened, his soul melted by their ringing voices, and he leapt up from his rowing-bench and sprang into the sea. Swimming through the dark waters, he climbed up on to the beach; and that would have been the end of him if laughter-loving Aphrodite had not pitied his youth and soft heart and carried him away to dwell with her in one of her sacred places. Grieving for the loss of their companion, the heroes went on their way.

And now to one side rose the steep rock of Scylla, and on the other Charybdis boiled and sputtered; but Thetis and her nymphs caught up the ship and tossed it from one to the next along the waves, as young girls play with a ball, and so they came safely through. And the nymphs dived back like seabirds to their homes under the water, while Scylla gnashed her ugly jaws at them.

Next they came to Scheria, the island of the good king Alcinoüs, ruler of the Phaeacians. There they met a great host of Colchians, still searching for Medea and afraid to go home without her; these demanded that Jason either give her up or prepare for battle. But Alcinoüs tried to pacify them, hoping the issue could be settled without bloodshed. And Medea sat at the feet of his queen Arete, and implored her not to let her be given up; and she implored the heroes too, for fear that in their weariness and longing for home they might forget their promises to her, stained with crime as she was. And each man among the Argonauts swore to protect her against an unjust judgement.

At night, when Alcinoüs lay on his couch thinking the matter over, his wife Arete pleaded with him for Medea: "for the maiden in the greatness of her suffering has broken my heart with her prayers." And Alcinoüs' heart was softened by the words of his wife, and he said to her, "Arete, you know I could drive the host of the Colchians from the island and defend the maiden with force; but I fear to do an injustice in the eyes of almighty Zeus. Hear, then, what I have decided. If Medea is still unmarried, then she is rightly under the authority of her father King Aietes, and to him she must return; but if on the journey Jason has already wedded her, then she shall go with him, for I will not separate a wife from her husband." So he spoke, and afterwards he fell asleep. Then Arete rose and sent a messenger to Jason, telling him Alcinoüs' judgement and advising him to marry Medea without delay. The messenger hastened to the heroes, and rejoicing they offered sacrifices and decked the bridal couch with the Golden Fleece, while Orpheus sang the marriage-song. And thus the marriage of Jason and Medea was accomplished, in fear as much as love, and not in the halls of Jason's father at home but hastily and in a foreign land. And in the morning Alcinoüs gave his judgement, and the Phaeacians came thronging to the ship bearing gifts for the new-wedded bride. As for the Colchians, they gave up their pursuit of Medea and never returned to face the anger of Aietes, but settled in the island.

Great labours were still in store for the heroes. Leaving Scheria, they were seized by the winds and carried into the gulf of Syrtis on the Libyan coast, where they were stranded among the shoals. For twelve days and twelve nights they carried the ship overland on their shoulders, and at last with the help of the gods they struck the open sea again. And now between them and the mainland of Hellas lay the island of Crete, guarded by Talos, the man of bronze.

There are two stories about Talos' origin. According to one, he was one of the many wonders created by the master-smith Hephaestus, like Aietes' brazen bulls and yoke of adamant. The other says that Talos was a survivor from the brazen race of men.

Whatever his origin, he was presented by Zeus to Europa to be the guardian of her Cretan island, and three times every day he walked all the way round it on his brazen feet, keeping watch. When he saw the Argo, he tore great handfuls of rocks out of the cliffside to cast at her. But Medea had a plan to overcome him. She knew the secret of his life: that while his whole body was bronze and invulnerable, all his blood was carried in a single vein that was plugged with a pin at the ankle. Calling to him sweetly, she told him that she was sent by the gods to reward his long service by drawing out the pin and replacing his blood with a magic ichor that would make him ageless and deathless for ever. The simple-minded giant let her approach and lull him to sleep; but once she had drawn out the pin and let all his blood run into the sand, she left him and he died. And so the Argonauts were able to take fresh water on board and continue on their way.

O, for Medea's wondrous alchemy,
Which wheresoe'er it fell made the earth gleam
With bright flowers, and the wintry boughs exhale
From vernal blooms fresh fragrance!

SHELLEY

At last Jason and his shipmates arrived back in Iolcos, where they were welcomed by Jason's ancient father Aeson. Pitying his father's age and weakness, Jason asked Medea if she knew any witchcraft powerful enough to restore his lost youth, and Medea agreed to try. That night, after offering prayers and sacrifices to her goddess Hecate, she brewed magic herbs in a cauldron, drained out the old man's blood, and filled his veins with her potion. Immediately his hair regained its colour and his flesh filled out, and he appeared before Jason as a young man again.

With this success behind her, Medea went to the palace of Pelias, claiming that she had quarrelled with her husband, and was kindly received by Pelias' daughters. Once she had their attention, she told them what she had been able to do for Jason's father, and offered to demonstrate her powers. She took an old ram, cut its throat, and threw its body into a cauldron together with the magical herbs, and in a moment a young lamb sprang out and ran away bleating.

Pelias' daughters were convinced, and they implored Medea to do the same for their old father. Medea consented, with some show of reluctance, and when the old man was sleeping, she directed them to cut up his body and drain out the blood. She then flung the pieces into the cauldron, but neglected to pronounce the proper spells over them, running instead to the palace tower to signal to Jason that he could now enter the city and seize the throne.

With Pelias' murder now added to their crimes, Jason and Medea were not allowed to rule very long in Iolcos before Pelias' son gathered a force together and drove them out.

Exiled, they wandered to Corinth, whose king took them in. And now Jason, weary of a wife so spotted with guilt, cast off Medea and made preparations to marry the young daughter of his host. Medea sent the maiden for a wedding-gift a poisoned robe: when she put it on it burned her to the bone, and her father, trying to help her, was consumed with her. To complete her vengeance, Medea then stabbed to death the children she had had by Jason, and fled away in a dragon-borne chariot sent by her dark protectress Hecate.

Jason's faith to Medea had long ago been sworn on the names of the gods, and from the day he broke it he was never lucky again. His later life was spent in wandering, without home or friends, until in old age he found himself once more at Corinth, sitting on the shore in the shadow of the Argo. As he sat there remembering the past, a piece from the stern crashed down, killing him in its fall. Afterwards the old ship disappeared from the harbour: Poseidon, the god of the sea, had carried it up and placed it among the stars.

BELLEROPHON AND PEGASUS

> *Up led by thee,*
> *Into the heaven of heavens I have presumed,*
> *An earthly guest, and drawn empyreal air,*
> *Thy temp'ring; with like safety guided down,*
> *Return me to my native element:*
> *Lest from this flying steed unreined (as once*
> *Bellerophon, though from a lower clime)*
> *Dismounted, on the Aleian field I fall,*
> *Erroneous there to wander and forlorn.*
>
> MILTON

The Corinthian prince Bellerophon, a grandson of the impious Sisyphus, had the misfortune to accidentally kill his brother.

Man and winged horse

Fleeing to Proetus, the king of Tiryns, for purification, Bellerophon was kindly received there. But Proetus' wife fell in love with him, and when he would not listen, she accused him privately to Proetus of having wronged her. As Bellerophon was his guest, Proetus was reluctant to commit any violent act against him; so he sent him to Iobates, the king of distant Lycia in the east, with a sealed letter of introduction. Iobates feasted Bellerophon royally for nine days, and on the tenth he asked to see the letter. There he read that Proetus wanted the young man killed.

No more anxious than Proetus to court Zeus' anger by treachery to a guest, Iobates thought of a way to accomplish the same end. He asked Bellerophon to kill for him a monster that was troubling the land: the Chimaera, which had a goat's body and a serpent for a tail and breathed forth flames from a lion's head. Bellerophon could not refuse. Consulting a seer, he was advised to catch the winged horse Pegasus, who had never been ridden or bridled. In fact the only work Pegasus had ever done was to strike a rock on the Muses' mountain

Helicon with his hoof, from whose imprint flowed a clear spring ever afterwards called Hippocrene, the Horse's Well.

With a magic bridle, the gift of Athene, Bellerophon was able to catch and tame the marvellous horse. That made his task easy: from Pegasus' back he shot the Chimaera without once coming close to its fiery breath. When he returned, Iobates sent him on other difficult missions, against a warrior tribe called the Solymi and then against the Amazons. These he accomplished successfully, with Pegasus' help. At last Iobates, convinced by Bellerophon's good fortune that he had been unjustly accused, gave up trying to kill him and married him to one of his daughters.

Bellerophon might have remained happily in Lycia and inherited the throne of Iobates, had it not been for his excessive ambition. Confident in the powers of Pegasus, he tried to ride him up Mount Olympus to the halls of the gods; but Zeus sent a gadfly that stung Pegasus, so that he reared and threw his rider back to earth. Pegasus finished the journey, and was received and stabled among the immortal horses of Zeus. Bellerophon, hated by the gods, wandered alone on the Aleian plain, gnawing at his own heart and shunning the paths of men until he died.

Chimaera

THESEUS

> *Whilom, as oldë stories tellen us,*
> *There was a duke that hightë Theseus.*
> *Of Athens he was lord and governour,*
> *And in his timë swich a conquerour*
> *That greater was there none under the sonnë.*
>
> CHAUCER

When Medea fled from Corinth to escape the wrath of Jason, her dragon-borne chariot carried her to Athens, ruled at the time by King Aegeus, who not only offered her hospitality but made her his wife.

Shortly afterwards, a stranger made his way to the court. Medea, suspecting him to be a pretender to the throne, mixed a poisonous cup of aconite and persuaded Aegeus to hand it to him. Just as the stranger was about to drink, Aegeus recognized the sword at his side and struck the cup out of his hand. This sword was one which he himself had left many years ago, together with a pair of sandals, under a large rock in Argolian Troezen across the Saronican Gulf, saying to the princess Aethra, "When your child becomes a man able to lift the rock, send him to me in Athens with these tokens and I shall acknowledge him as my son."

This stranger was indeed Aegeus' son Theseus. Leaving his mother Aethra, he had set out for Athens overland, by the long way round, hoping to meet adventures along the road. The land route to Athens was infested with robbers and murderers who preyed on all who travelled it, and Theseus meant to clear the way of them.

The first he met was Corynetes, the Cudgeller, who used to knock travellers' brains out with a huge brazen club: Theseus snatched it from him and served him the same way. The next was Sinis, nicknamed Pityocamptes, the Pine-bender, who tied all he caught to two pine-trees bent down to the ground, and then released them so that his victim was torn apart: he too was done by as he did. Next came Sciron, who forced passing travellers to wash his feet for him and then as they bent over kicked them over the cliff's edge into the sea, where lived a man-eating turtle who finished them off. Him Theseus presented to his old dependent the turtle. The last bandit Theseus met was one Procrustes, who invited all travellers to pass the night at his house. He had a remarkable bed, which his guests always found either too long or too short. Procrustes would force them to lie down, and then either stretch them or trim them till they fitted it exactly, the treatment being always fatal. Now at last the maker of the murderous bed was made to lie on it, and that was the end of him.

When Theseus was welcomed to Aegeus' palace, he learned of the troubles of the kingdom. The first was that Aegeus' brother and his fifty sons, who had always disputed Aegeus' right to reign in Athens, were just now plotting to overthrow him. Theseus led his father's forces against them in battle, and compelled them to sue for peace. The second evil had its origin in an event of some years before, when Minos, son of Europa and king of the ancient kingdom of Crete, had sent his son Androgeus to the Panathenaic games. Androgeus won every trophy that was offered, and Aegeus, fearing the friendship of this powerful prince with his conspiring nephews, had him ambushed and killed. Minos demanded that the Athenians in reparation should annually send to Crete seven youths and seven maidens to be delivered to the Minotaur.

Now the Minotaur was a monster, having the body of a man and the head of a bull, that had been born to Minos' queen in punishment for an offence committed by Minos against the gods. Wanting to hide the shame of such a child, Minos had commanded the cunning craftsman Daedalus to design a mysterious building, full of winding passages and known as the Labyrinth, in the middle of which the Minotaur had his den. The labyrinth was built in such a way that the single entrance, once passed, was impossible to find again, so that even if one of the young victims managed to escape the monster he would certainly die of hunger and exhaustion before he could ever find his way back to the light.

> *His waxen wings did mount above his reach,*
> *And melting heavens conspired his overthrow.*
> CHRISTOPHER MARLOWE

Daedalus, the master-craftsman who built the labyrinth, learned his skills from Athene, the patroness of handwork of all kinds. Born in Athens, he was banished from his native city for murdering one of his apprentices, a young craftsman whose skill threatened to rival his own. Daedalus sought refuge at the court of Minos, who welcomed him for his wonderful abilities. After he had made for Minos not only the labyrinth but many other marvels, Daedalus wanted to leave Crete; but Minos refused to let him go, some say locking him up in the labyrinth he had designed. Daedalus' ingenuity showed him a way of escape. He fashioned two pairs of great wings, one for himself and one for his son Icarus. As he fastened the wings to his son's shoulders, he warned him not to rise too high, for fear the sun would melt the wax holding the pinions together. But Icarus, enraptured with the new experience of flying, disobeyed and mounted up towards the sun, whereupon his wings fell apart and he plunged into the sea and was drowned. His father sorrowfully carried his body for burial to a nearby island, since called Icaria.

Daedalus was kindly received by King Cocalus of Sicily. Meanwhile Minos, determined not to lose the most valuable of his servants, travelled all over the Mediterranean in search of him. He took with him a spiral shell, offering a large reward to anyone who could pass a linen thread through it, there being only one man in the world equal to such a problem. Cocalus undertook to get the shell threaded, and handed it to Daedalus. Drilling the shell at the top, Daedalus tied a strand of gossamer to the leg of an ant, which he induced up through the whorls by smearing honey around the drilled hole. Then he joined the linen thread to the end of the gossamer and drew it through. Cocalus returned the shell and claimed the reward: Minos replied that Cocalus was certainly sheltering his runaway servant and must give him up. The daughters of Cocalus, for whom Daedalus had made ingenious toys, contrived at this point to boil Minos to death in his bath, so that Daedalus was able to stay in Sicily for the rest of his life. Minos and his brother Rhadamanthus, as Zeus' sons by Europa, were honoured in the underworld by being made the judges of the dead.

Minotaur

Thou mayst not wander in that labyrinth;
There Minotaurs and ugly treasons lurk.

SHAKESPEARE

Soon after Theseus' arrival in Athens, and before Minos set off again in search of Daedalus, the tribute again fell due and the fourteen youths and maidens were chosen by lot. In

spite of his father's pleading, Theseus resolved to go as one of
their number. When the ship carrying the victims was crossing
over to Crete, King Minos, who had come along to supervise,
boasted to Theseus of being a son of Zeus. "Prove it!" said
Theseus; whereupon Minos raised his hands and prayed to
Zeus, who answered with a roll of thunder out of a clear sky.
Minos then challenged Theseus' own powers by throwing his
gold signet-ring into the sea and ordering the hero to retrieve
it. Theseus dived over the side, was escorted to the bottom
by a school of dolphins, and received the ring back from
Amphitrite, the wife of Poseidon, god of the sea; then he swam
back up and returned it to King Minos.

Having arrived in Crete, Theseus gained the love of Minos'
daughter Ariadne, who offered to help him overcome her
beast-formed brother if he would take her back to Athens and
marry her. The help she gave him was a ball of twine and the
knowledge of how to use it. When he entered the labyrinth,
he tied the end of the thread to the doorpost, unwinding it as
he walked on, so that at any time he could find his way back
by rolling up the clew. Deeper and deeper he went into the
mysterious network of paths, until scattered bones and a
smell of filth and decay warned him that he was near the
Minotaur's den. Suddenly from the central darkness the
monster came charging at him. Theseus drew a short sword,
the gift of Ariadne, and stepping aside, struck at him as he
passed. Wounded and bellowing, the monster turned on him.
This time Theseus was able to despatch him, driving the sword
through his body and then cutting off his head.

With the Minotaur dead, Theseus still had to escape from
the labyrinth. Winding up the thread in his hand, he soon
retraced the path to the entrance where Ariadne was waiting
for him. Meanwhile she had overpowered the guards with
drugged wine and released the other prisoners; and together
they all fled to the ship and set sail for Athens.

Paint me a cavernous waste shore
Cast in the unstilled Cyclades,
Paint me the bold anfractuous rocks
Faced by the snarled and yelping seas.

Display me Aeolus above
Reviewing the insurgent gales
Which tangle Ariadne's hair
And swell with haste the perjured sails.

T. S. ELIOT

On the way up the eastern coast of Greece, the company disembarked for a day or two on the island of Naxos; and when Theseus sailed away, he left Ariadne sleeping on the shore. Why this treachery to her, no one knows. She awoke just in time to see the ship departing over the horizon, and began to shriek aloud in grief and terror. At that moment it happily chanced that the wine-god Dionysus came by, with his laughing and singing companions, and took the forsaken maiden to be his bride, setting on her head a marvellous crown. His bridal gift to her can be seen now among the stars: we call it the constellation Corona Borealis.

When the ship with the fourteen victims had set out all those weeks ago from Athens, it carried a black sail in token of mourning. Aegeus gave his son on leaving a white sail to hoist, if he ever returned, as a signal of his success. In the haste and excitement of the return, Theseus forgot to hoist the white sail and entered the harbour at Athens under the black one. His old father was watching for the ship on Cape Sunium, the southernmost point of Attica, and seeing it enter the Saronican Gulf under the signal of mourning, he lost all hope and threw himself into the sea, which to this day is called the Aegean after him.

Theseus' heroic career did not end with his becoming king of Athens in his father's place. He is honoured by the

Athenians as the first man to bring all the people of Attica together under one strong rule, and as having then dissolved the kingdom and established a commonwealth. During his reign at Athens, the district of Attica was invaded by the Amazons, a tribe of warrior-women from the east. Theseus defeated them and married their queen Hippolyta, who bore him a son, Hippolytus.

> *Like as the cursèd son of Theseus,*
> *That, following his chase in dewy morn,*
> *To fly his stepdame's love outrageous,*
> *Of his own steeds was all to pieces torn,*
> *And his fair limbs left in the woods forlorn;*
> *That for his sake Diana did lament,*
> *And all the woody nymphs did wail and mourn.*
>
> SPENSER

After some years Hippolyta died and Theseus married Phaedra, the sister of a friendly king. Meanwhile his son Hippolytus was growing up into a fine young man, devoted to hunting and to Artemis, the maiden goddess of the chase. Because Hippolytus had no use for her and her ways, the love-goddess Aphrodite swore vengeance, which she accomplished by making his stepmother Phaedra fall in love with him. Hippolytus would have nothing to do with her, and her love soon turned to hatred. She hanged herself in despair in her royal apartment, leaving a letter that falsely declared her death was due to the shame of being secretly wooed by her husband's son. Now it was Theseus' turn to swear revenge against Hippolytus, and he uttered a curse on him and sent him into banishment. As Hippolytus was driving away from Athens, dashing in his chariot along the shore, Poseidon sent to meet him a huge sea-monster, which so terrified his horses that they bolted, and he was thrown from his chariot and killed. His friend Artemis then told the truth to Theseus, who would have given all he possessed to turn against himself the hasty curse: but in vain.

The Romans have a tradition about the fate of Hippolytus. Artemis, deeply grieved at the death of her favourite, appealed to the divinely gifted healer Asclepius, the son of Apollo and trained by Cheiron. He allowed himself to be persuaded, and restored Hippolytus to life. But Hades and the three Fates, alarmed at what might happen if a mortal healer could go on snatching their subjects from them, made Zeus destroy Asclepius with a thunderbolt. Artemis, however, had got what she wanted. Wrapping Hippolytus in a thick cloud, she transported him to her sacred grove of Nemi at Aricia in Italy, a mysterious place beside a dark, cliff-surrounded lake, where he went on living under the Latin name of Virbius, married to the nymph Egeria.

This Arician grove of Artemis, or Diana, as the Romans called her, was ruled by a curious custom. Besides the immortal Virbius and his divine consort, the grove was inhabited by a solitary mortal, its priest, who was known as "the king of the wood". This man was always one who had first come there as a runaway slave, seeking sanctuary. In the grove, which was of oak-trees, there was one tree among whose dark foliage shone a single bough of gold. This the fugitive had to break off as a ritual act of challenge: he would then fight for the priesthood with whoever was the priest at the time. The fight was always to the death: the winner held the priesthood as his right until challenged and killed in his turn.

Facilis descensus Averno . . .
Sed revocare gradum superasque evadere ad auras,
Hoc opus, hic labor est.

VERGIL

(The descent to Avernus is easy; but to retrace your way and escape to the upper world, that is the difficulty.)

Besides the Amazons, other invaders of Attica were the tribe of the Lapiths under King Peirithoüs. Trying to drive off a herd of cattle, these were indignantly pursued by Theseus. When he caught up with Peirithoüs, who turned to face him, each was so impressed with the other's strength and courage that they forthwith swore to be friends whatever might happen.

After the death of Phaedra, Peirithoüs being also without a wife, the two friends agreed to make an expedition together to Sparta and carry off the little princess Helen, the daughter of the Spartan queen Leda by Zeus, who had visited her in the form of a swan. Though still a very young girl, Helen already gave promise of becoming the most beautiful woman in the world. The agreement was that after capturing her they would draw lots for her, and the winner would help the loser to carry off as his bride some other one of Zeus' daughters. Theseus having won Helen, he and Peirithoüs descended to Tartarus in an effort to steal away Persephone, the queen of the underworld. Hades welcomed the pair as his guests and invited them to be seated, but the seat he offered them was a very odd one called the Chair of Forgetfulness, and it held them fast. There they sat on and on, until many years later Heracles came down to the lower world to fetch up Cerberus: Theseus he pulled free by main force, but the chair would not release Peirithoüs, the leader of the raid, who is sitting there still.

While Theseus was held a prisoner in the house of Hades, Helen's twin brothers Castor and Polydeuces rescued her and took her home to Sparta, and with her they took Theseus' mother Aethra to be Helen's slave. On Theseus' return to Athens he found not only his mother and his bride gone but many things changed and the kingdom in disorder; and, weakened as he was by his sufferings, he decided to leave rather than reclaim his throne. His travels brought him to the island of Scyros, where the reigning king, the friend of an old enemy, murdered Theseus by pushing him over a cliff.

Many generations after the death of Theseus, the Athenians fought a critical battle against the Persians on the field of Marathon; and the ghost of Theseus came up out of the ground in the thick of the fight, swinging the brazen club that the hero in his first adventure took from the bandit Corynetes. Years later on the island of Scyros was found a stone coffin containing the skeleton of a giant man along with some weapons of bronze. The bones were revered as those of Theseus and carried back with rejoicing to Athens, where the temple built to house them, the Theseion, may still be seen.

Labyrinth.

V

THE ROYAL HOUSE
OF THEBES

THE CHILDREN OF AGENOR

> *Or sweet Europa's mantle blew unclasp'd,*
> *From off her shoulder backward borne:*
> *From one hand droop'd a crocus: one hand grasp'd*
> *The mild bull's golden horn.*
>
> TENNYSON

KING Agenor of Tyre had among his children a daughter
called Europa and a son called Cadmus. Europa was so
charming a maiden that she won the heart of Zeus himself.
Happening to see her once when looking down to earth, he

Illustration: Europa and the Bull

laid a plan to carry her off. While she was playing with other young girls beside the seashore, he turned himself into a milk-white bull with golden horns, so gentle and playful that the princess came fearlessly up to him and decked him with the flowers she was gathering. She put out her hands and patted his neck, and even mounted on his back: whereupon he immediately sprang up from the grass, dashed out over the yellow sands and plunged into the sea, swimming far out of sight of the maidens left shrieking on the shore. The terrified princess dropped her flowers and clung to him, crying for help all the time. On they rushed through the sea, with Europa's veil blowing out behind her. At last Zeus brought her ashore in the meadows of Crete, where he calmed her fears and promised her that the whole continent should be called Europe after her, and her children should be kings.

Meanwhile Europa's family were greatly distressed. King Agenor sent his son Cadmus out to find her, warning him not to come home if he failed. In his wanderings Cadmus crossed the sea and came to Apollo's oracle at Delphi, where he asked for advice. Apollo told him: "Travel till you meet a heifer that has never been harnessed to the plough. Follow wherever she leads you, and note the first place where she lies down: there build yourself a city, and call the district Boeotia (Cow-land)."

Cadmus and his friends kept on until they met the heifer, who led them on for some time before she at length lay down to rest. Cadmus gave thanks and sent his companions into the woods to fetch water to pour out with offerings to the gods. Deep in the wood they found a spring with a cave beside it. As soon as they began to draw water, a vast serpent crawled out of the cave and attacked them: some it poisoned, some it crushed, until none was left alive. Tired of waiting, Cadmus came in search of them, only to see the serpent crawling over the bodies of the dead and drinking blood from their wounds. Furiously he threw his javelin at it and pierced its throat. It struggled and thrashed wildly about, but finally grew weak and sank to the ground.

While Cadmus watched its dying struggles, a voice came out of the wood announcing that he had grievously offended the war-god Ares by killing the serpent that was under his protection. Immediately Cadmus' protectress Athene appeared, commanding him to plough up the earth and sow in the furrows the serpent's teeth. As soon as he did so, there sprang up a crop of armed men, who began to quarrel and fight desperately among themselves until all but five lay dead; and with the help of these five men Cadmus founded his city of Thebes. In time he married Harmonia, a daughter of Ares, whose anger was somewhat appeased by the death of the earth-born men.

ZEUS AND SEMELE

> *Brighter art thou than flaming Jupiter*
> *When he appeared to hapless Semele.*
> CHRISTOPHER MARLOWE

Whether or not because of Ares' displeasure, many misfortunes befell the house of Cadmus. He and Harmonia had four daughters and a son, all of whose families felt the anger of the gods.

One of the daughters, Semele, was beloved and visited by Zeus, who left her pregnant with a divine child. Before the child was to be born, Zeus' jealous wife Hera, disguised as an old woman, tempted the princess by playing on her curiosity. "If your lover really is the father of gods and men, why does he not appear to you in his full glory, as he does to his divine consort?" Semele then began to tease her lover, until Zeus, wearied, came to her brandishing his thunderbolts and in the full blaze of his majesty, so that she was instantly burnt up. Zeus snatched the child from the ashes and sewed him up in his thigh until he was ready to be born. For this reason the young god Dionysus was known as "the twice-born", or "he of the double door". One of his deeds in later life was to descend to the underworld and rescue his mother Semele, whom he introduced with divine honours into Olympus.

INO AND ATHAMAS

By Leucothea's lovely hands,
And her son that rules the strands . . .

MILTON

Cadmus' second daughter Ino married King Athamas of Boeotia and plotted the death of Phrixus and Helle, his children by a former wife. When he found out her wickedness, Athamas turned against her and the children she had borne him, stabbing the elder in a fit of madness. Ino seized her younger son and fled, finally leaping into the sea with him to escape Athamas' rage. Zeus turned them both into divinities of the sea, under the changed names of Leucothea and Palaemon.

PENTHEUS

Bacchus, that first from out the purple grape
Crushed the sweet poison of misusèd wine . . .

MILTON

The third daughter had a son named Pentheus who ruled over Thebes in his grandfather's place. During his reign the god Dionysus returned to Thebes from his long journeyings in the

east. Now Dionysus had for his province the vine with its fruits
and their products, and he was worshipped appropriately with
ecstatic singing and dancing. The people of Thebes rushed out
of doors to join the throngs of Maenads, his frenzied women
worshippers who roamed about the hills dressed in fawn-skins
and carrying the thyrsus in his honour. Pentheus, though
warned not to meddle by the old blind prophet Teiresias,
spoke out strongly against these practices and even tried to
capture the god. Dionysus sent madness on his mother, who
was roaming about with the rest, so that she thought her son a
wild beast and tore him apart with her bare hands, helped by
the other women.

ACTAEON

> *I would I were Actaeon, whom Diana did disguise,*
> *To walk the woods unknown whereas my lady lies:*
> *A hart of pleasant hue I wish that I were so,*
> *So that my lady knew alone me and no mo.*
>
> *The shaling nuts and mast that falleth from the tree*
> *Should serve for my repast, might I my lady see;*
> *Sometime that I might say when I saw her alone,*
> *"Behold thy slave, alone, that walks these woods*
> *   unknown!"*

ANON.

Cadmus' remaining daughter was the mother of Actaeon, a
young huntsman who had the misfortune one day while
hunting to come upon a pool which was a favourite retreat of
the huntress-goddess Artemis. The goddess was just then
bathing there, surrounded by all the nymphs, who had laid
aside their bows and quivers and were refreshing themselves
in the heat of the day. As soon as they saw the startled intruder,

they all drew together to protect their mistress, while she stood up in the midst of them and uttered a few angry words, at the same time splashing him with water. Immediately the rash Actaeon felt a change come over him. His limbs lengthened and were covered with a brown coat, and horns began to sprout from his forehead: in no time he had become a fine stag, like the very ones he had taken such pleasure in hunting. As soon as his hounds saw him, they started off in fierce pursuit. Their master tried to call out to them, but his voice was no longer his own: all that could be heard among the barking of the hounds was the panting of an exhausted stag. The chase lasted only a short time. Actaeon was pulled down by his own hounds, in fearful punishment for disturbing the retreat of the goddess Artemis.

OEDIPUS

> *Although a subtler Sphinx renew*
> *Riddles of death Thebes never knew.*
>
> SHELLEY

The only son of Cadmus had a grandson, Laius, who became king of Thebes and married his cousin Jocasta. Laius was warned by the Delphic oracle that the son he longed for would be his murderer. When the baby was born, Laius bound his feet tightly together and commanded a shepherd to leave him on the mountain-side to die. Instead, the shepherd gave him to a herdsman from Corinth, telling him to take the baby far away. The herdsman carried him to the Corinthian court, where the king and queen, having no children of their own, adopted him. They called him Oedipus, from his bruised and swollen feet.

When he reached manhood, Oedipus asked the Delphic

oracle what the future held for him, and learned to his horror that he was fated to kill his father and marry his mother. Turning his face from Corinth and his supposed parents, he took the road towards Thebes in the east. In a narrow mountain pass he met an old man in a chariot, driving furiously towards Delphi. Ordered to stand aside, Oedipus kept straight on:

Oedipus and the Sphinx

when the old man struck at him, Oedipus knocked him into the roadway to be trampled by the horses. Then he fought and killed all his attendants but one, who fled back to Thebes with the news that King Laius was dead.

Thebes at this time was troubled by a ravaging monster, the Sphinx, whose body was that of a winged lion with the head and breast of a woman. Lying in wait for travellers, she put to all she caught the following riddle: "What is it that goes in the morning on four feet, at noonday on two, on three in the evening?" None being able to answer, she throttled and devoured them all. It was to consult the god about this pest that Laius had set out for Delphi.

Continuing along the way to Thebes, Oedipus was met by the Sphinx, who posed him her riddle. Without hesitating he replied, "Man: in the morning of life he goes on all fours, in maturity on his two feet, in old age leaning on a staff." The Sphinx in her mortification flung herself off a cliff. Rid of her hateful presence, the Thebans rewarded Oedipus with the kingdom and the hand of its widowed queen Jocasta.

For several years Oedipus lived happily with Jocasta, who bore him two sons and two daughters. But the people suffered for the unknown guilt of their king, being visited with famine and plague. The Delphic oracle, consulted, ordered the Thebans to cast out from their gates the murderer of Laius. When search failed to find the man, Oedipus pronounced on him, whoever he might be, a dreadful curse; then he sent for Teiresias, by now very old, to ask what he knew of the matter. Teiresias, seeing that the truth could only cause more suffering, refused to answer: Oedipus in his own blindness sent him away with insults and threats.

When in spite of such a warning Oedipus continued the search, the truth began to be uncovered. From all the accounts of Laius' death, he realized that this was the old man he had killed near Delphi, and that he had thus pronounced the curse against himself. Worse was to follow. The king of Corinth died, and Oedipus in the midst of his grief rejoiced that he had not brought about his father's death. The Corinthian messenger checked him: "But you were his adopted child: it was I myself who brought you to him, a helpless baby given to me by a shepherd of King Laius."

Then at last it was clear that Oedipus was indeed the murderer of his father and the husband of his own mother, the man whose guilt polluted the city. Jocasta in horror hanged herself from a beam of the palace, while Oedipus put out his eyes and wandered in exile from Thebes, leaning on his faithful daughter Antigone. After long journeyings he came to the grove of Colonus in Attica, where the gods forgave him and he died. Thebes meanwhile was ruled by Jocasta's brother Creon.

When Oedipus' two sons Eteocles and Polynices reached manhood, they arranged that they would rule for alternate years. Eteocles began, and at the end of his first term showed no intention of ever giving up the kingdom; whereupon his brother gathered six powerful friends with their armies and the seven contingents marched against Thebes. In the battle each of the brothers gave the other his death-wound, so that sad Creon was once more left in power. He decreed that the body of Eteocles should be buried with funeral honours, while that of Polynices should be left outside the gate for carrion beasts and birds. This was more than an insult, because while a body lay unburied the ghost could not cross the river of death but wandered miserably up and down the shore. Antigone dared to cover her brother's body with earth, and Creon, afraid of disorder in the state if her action went unpunished, had her walled up alive in a tomb. "Life for life," Teiresias had warned him; and now Creon's son Haemon, who was to have married Antigone, died by his own hand. Thus all the children of Oedipus perished through family dissension, except for the younger daughter, who refused to help her sister. The story does not tell what became of her.

E p i s

VI. THE TALE OF TROY

THE APPLE OF DISCORD

> *The Abominable, that uninvited came*
> *Into the fair Peleian banquet-hall,*
> *And cast the golden fruit upon the board,*
> *And bred this change ...*
>
> TENNYSON

THE story of the ten-years' struggle at Troy begins a generation before the war broke out, with the wedding of Peleus and
Thetis, the destined parents of the hero Achilles. All the
Olympians and the lesser gods came to do them honour, all
but Eris, the hateful goddess of discord, who was not invited.
But Eris stole in unnoticed, and she threw down on the long
banqueting-table a golden apple inscribed "For the fairest".

Illustration: Eris

Three of the lady goddesses, Hera, Athene and Aphrodite, immediately began wrangling over it, and Father Zeus, who deals justice to gods and men, was appealed to for a decision. Zeus, fearing the ill will of the losers, commanded Hermes the divine messenger to lead the three to Mount Ida in Phrygia where the shepherd Paris was tending his flocks, and there let him decide.

Now Paris was the son of King Priam of Troy and his wife Hecabe, and at his birth his mother had a dream in which she brought forth a fire-brand, interpreted by the seers to mean that the young prince was to be his country's downfall. Priam in alarm gave him to his chief herdsman to take away and kill; but the man brought back false proofs of the child's death and brought him up unknown as his own son. Paris lived the life of a simple shepherd, happy in the love of the fountain-nymph Oenone.

Into this pastoral solitude came Hermes and the rival goddesses. Seeing that Paris was abashed and bewildered at the sight of so much divine beauty being paraded before him, each offered him a gift if he would award the prize to her. Hera promised power and honour, Athene victory in war, and Aphrodite the hand of Helen of Sparta, the daughter of Zeus and the loveliest of mortal women. At the mention of Helen's name, Paris immediately forgot about everything else, even his sweetheart Oenone, and he gave Aphrodite the apple, thus making Hera and Athene his eternal enemies.

Shortly after this, public games were to be held at Priam's court, and Paris persuaded his foster-father to accompany him there. Once arrived at Troy, Paris insisted on competing. He won all the events, defeating among others Priam's other sons, whose jealousy was so great that they resolved to kill him. They blocked off the exits from the arena and all attacked him at once with their swords. Priam's herdsman, to save Paris's life, sprang forward and declared to the king who the young man was. Priam received his son with great rejoicing, the fatal oracle never once entering his mind.

Paris, remembering the love-goddess's promise to him, soon found a pretext to go and visit King Menelaus of Sparta, to whom the beautiful Helen was married. He repaid Menelaus' hospitality by carrying off his wife and many treasures from the palace and sailing with his booty straight back to Troy. There Helen was warmly welcomed for her exquisite grace and charm, and amid public celebrations Paris married her.

Helen's husband Menelaus had been one of many suitors to ask for her hand. For fear that strife would break out when she made her choice, the husband of her mother Leda had required all the suitors to swear to accept her decision and to defend the man she chose against anyone who might try to take her from him. Now Menelaus, finding Helen gone, hastened to Mycenae to his brother Agamemnon, and the two of them sent messengers to all the princes of Greece who had been her suitors and had taken the oath. Menelaus went himself to Ithaca to appeal to its king Odysseus, famous for his cunning.

Now Odysseus had been warned by an oracle that if he went to Troy he would be away twenty years and then return a poor man and friendless; and he resolved to feign madness rather than go. Menelaus found him in the fields, in a peasant's cap, furiously ploughing with an ox and an ass yoked together and sowing the furrows with salt. Snatching Odysseus' little son from his mother's arms, Menelaus laid him down just in front of the team, so that Odysseus had to rein them back quickly to avoid trampling him. "Aha!" exclaimed Menelaus, "there's a man with his wits about him!" Having been found out, Odysseus could not in honour refuse; so he sadly left his wife Penelope and the young Telemachus to join the expedition.

The other hero whose services the brothers were most anxious to secure was Achilles, the son of the mortal Peleus and the sea-goddess Thetis. Not only was he a great champion, but an oracle had declared that Troy could never be taken without his help.

When Achilles was born, Thetis had resolved to make him immortal like herself. According to one story, she dipped him in the deadly underground river Styx to make his body invulnerable, so that the only place that could still be wounded was the spot at the heel by which she held him. The other story is that Peleus caught her trying to burn away Achilles' mortal nature in the fire, as Demeter did with the child of Celeus. When Peleus interfered, Thetis was so angry that she left him forever and went back to her home in the sea; but she continued to watch over the fortunes of her son.

Peleus took his motherless child to the cave of Cheiron to be educated, and there Achilles quickly surpassed all the sons of the heroes in running, wrestling and hunting. Thetis, watching from her far-off home, was grieved to see him excel. She knew that he was destined either to live a most glorious life and die young or to live long but obscurely; and naturally she wanted to lengthen his life. For this reason she disguised him as a girl and sent him to live among the maidens at the court of a friendly king. Here Odysseus now came to seek him out. Arrived at the palace, he displayed a huge chest of gifts, most of them dresses and jewels, from which the ladies were invited to choose for themselves. When one among them gave a loud cry and seized a shield and spear from the heap, Odysseus recognized his man, who was easily persuaded to take up a warrior's life and join Agamemnon's force. With Achilles went his cousin and friend Patroclus.

Other famous leaders of the army were the brave but foolhardy Ajax, Diomedes the Argive, and the old king Nestor of Pylus, renowned for his wisdom and his gift of persuasive speech, who had ruled over three generations of men. With them also went Calchas the seer, a Trojan priest of Apollo who had forsaken his own people to help the Greek cause.

THE WAR

> *Was this the face that launched a thousand ships*
> *And burnt the topless towers of Ilium?*
>
> CHRISTOPHER MARLOWE

The Greek fleet gathered at Aulis in Boeotia, where for several days contrary winds forced them to remain in harbour. Calchas, who had already prophesied to the army that they would spend nine years besieging Troy and take it only in the tenth, now declared that the goddess Artemis was angry and could be appeased only by the death of Agamemnon's daughter Iphigeneia. To this Agamemnon sorrowfully consented. To get the girl away from her mother Clytemnestra, he sent a message that the princess was to come to Aulis to be married to Achilles, and Clytemnestra sent her gladly, decked in her wedding-garments. There she was sacrificed, the gale dropped, and the fleet set out on its north-east course across the Aegean. But some say that Artemis accepted the maiden's dutifulness instead of her life and before the knife could fall, carried her away wrapped in a cloud to Tauris, to serve as her priestess.

The fleet put ashore briefly at Tenedos, where the famous archer Philoctetes was bitten in the foot by a serpent so venomous that the wound could not be cured, but festered and stank intolerably. Since no one could bear to be near him, his companions left him on a small rocky island, where he kept himself miserably alive on what he could shoot.

Arriving at Troy, the Greeks drew their ships up on to the shore, set up their camp, and proceeded to lay siege to the city. And there for weeks and months and years they remained. The struggle dragged out to nine years: King Priam and the Trojans would not surrender, and Agamemnon with his forces would not go away. The army was weary and homesick, and in the tenth year Apollo became angered and took up his stand beside the ships, shooting arrows of pestilence day after day into the Greek camp. At the same time Achilles quarrelled with Agamemnon over a captive woman and withdrew from the fighting to his tent, where he sat brooding. The Trojans, seeing division in the enemy camp, attacked with such spirit that Agamemnon quickly arranged a truce, during which Paris and Menelaus were to fight it out, man to man, for fair Helen. But nothing was to be decided by this means; for Aphrodite, when she saw that Menelaus was winning, wrapped a cloud around her favourite Paris and bore him away from the field back to his house in Troy.

Agamemnon, Odysseus and their friends did their best to placate the wrathful Achilles, but to no avail. Meanwhile his friend Patroclus day after day went out to battle in Achilles' armour and fought brilliantly, until Apollo himself disabled him, and he was then easily killed by the bravest of Troy's defenders, Priam's son Hector, who stripped him of the armour as his rightful prize. When the news was brought to Achilles, he almost went mad with grief: he forgot his anger against the Greek leaders and swore to re-enter the conflict and avenge his friend. His mother Thetis and her attendant sea-nymphs came up out of the sea to comfort him, walking in a long line across the sands to his tent. Hearing him swear to kill Hector, she warned him that Hector's death must soon be followed by his own; but he thought little of that, and she went sadly away, promising to bring him new armour, which she would persuade the smith-god Hephaestus to forge. Meanwhile Achilles, unarmed as he was, hastened to help the Greeks defend the body of Patroclus, which the exulting Trojans were trying to drag back to the city, to dishonour it and expose it on the city wall. Standing at the trench that bounded the camp, he shouted aloud three times, with such a trumpet-sound that the Trojan horses wheeled round in confusion. Twelve of the Trojan nobles were thrown and crushed by their own chariot-wheels, while the rest scattered in flight and Achilles bore away the body of his friend.

On high Olympus, Hephaestus sponged the workshop grime from his face and arms and received the goddess Thetis into his house of marvels. Here she was always honoured and welcome; for many years ago she had taken him in and sheltered him after his fall from heaven. Glad that she now called on his skill, he promised her what she asked, "and would that I could keep your son from death's sight in the evil day, as easily as I can make him armour that will amaze the eyes of men."

> *The wrath*
> *Of stern Achilles on his foe pursued*
> *Thrice fugitive about Troy wall.*
> MILTON

The finished armour that Thetis brought to Achilles was of the finest craftsmanship, in copper and tin and silver and gold. Most splendid of the pieces was the shield, on which the divine smith had pictured the stars of heaven and scenes of earthly life, of peace and war, city and country, the whole encircled by the stream of Oceanus that girdles the world. Achilles rejoiced when he saw the armour. Calling the leaders of the army together, he made up his quarrel with them; then he armed himself and went furiously out to battle. As his charioteer guided them along, Achilles spoke to his horses, saying, "When we finish this day's fighting, mind you bring me safely back to the camp, not leave me dead on the plain as you did Patroclus." His horse Xanthus bowed his head and spoke: "Mighty Achilles, today we shall bring you back safe, but your evil day is near, brought on by heaven and stern Fate, and not by any fault of ours." The Fates would not let him say more, and Achilles grieving replied, "Xanthus, why do you foretell my death? I know that I shall fall here, far from my dear father and mother; but I will not leave the field till I have given the Trojans their fill of fighting." And he urged the horses forward with a shout.

Achilles made havoc among the Trojan host till the river Scamander was choked with corpses and red with blood. In anger the river-god spoke from his channel and asked him at least to do his killing on land; and when Achilles was slow to comply, Scamander rose from his banks and chased him along the plain, roaring to Simois his brother flood to join him. Hera, to help Achilles, sent her son Hephaestus to drive Scamander back with fire. When the river rushed boiling down into his bed she called out, "Now hold back your flames: it is not fitting for us to use such violence against a god for the sake of mortal men."

King Priam, watching from the city wall, saw how the Trojans were falling before Achilles, and he commanded that the gates should be opened to give them refuge. They came crowding through in panic, flying like a herd of deer before Achilles, who was half mad with vengeful battle-lust and the thirst of glory. Soon all the Trojans were safe in the city, all but Hector, who, heedless of his friends' entreaties to come inside, waited for Achilles before the gates.

The weighing of dooms

When Achilles bore down on him, his armour flashing, raging like the war-god Ares himself, Hector's courage failed him and he fled in dismay, three times circling the city walls with Achilles after him. So evenly matched were the runners that it was like a pursuit in a dream, where one cannot escape nor the other overtake; for neither could Achilles catch up with Hector nor Hector break away from Achilles. Even so, Hector might yet have saved his life by his speed, if Fate had not decided otherwise. On the summit of Olympus, Zeus took up his golden scales. He placed a doom on each side, one for Achilles and one for Hector, and Hector's fell down towards the realm of Hades while that of Achilles flew up and kicked the beam. When he saw that, Hector's protector Apollo, who had hitherto kept up his strength and nerved his running, left him.

Now for the fourth time they were passing the twin springs of the Scamander and the stone troughs where in peace-time the Trojan women brought their washing, when Athene, always friendly to Achilles, resolved to make Hector fight. She assumed the form of his favourite brother Deïphobus and hastened up to him, saying: "I have stayed outside the wall for your sake: now let us make a stand together against the fierce Achilles." With these words she persuaded him to turn and face Achilles; but when the two met, Hector, looking round for his brother, saw how he had been tricked. "Oh, shame!" he cried out, "the gods have betrayed me to my doom: then let me not die without a struggle, but fight so that those who come after may remember me."

Hector then charged down on Achilles with all his force, while Achilles watched closely for a place to strike. As he came on, Achilles drove his spear through the base of his throat, where the armour taken from Patroclus did not protect him. Hector fell, and as his strength flowed from him he implored Achilles to accept whatever ransom the Trojans

would offer for his body, so that it might be buried at home
with due rites: this Achilles refused. Then Hector said with his
last breath, "I know what you are, iron-hearted man whom
prayers cannot soften. But see that your treatment of me does
not move the gods to vengeance, in the day when Paris and
Apollo shall cut you down beside the Scaean Gate." As he
spoke, the shades of death enfolded him, and his soul went
down lamenting to the house of Hades. And Achilles replied
to the dead body: "It is over for you; as for me, I will accept
my fate whenever the gods see fit to send it." Then he attached
the body by the ankles to the back of his chariot and dragged
it through the dust towards the ships, while all the Trojans
watching from the wall bewailed the death of their champion.
They mourned for Hector, but it was for themselves that they
lamented; for they saw approaching their own evil day.

Having killed Hector, Achilles now held Patroclus' funeral,
burning his body on a pyre along with dogs, horses and Trojan
captives slaughtered in his honour, and raising a tomb over
the remains. Round the tomb he daily dragged the body of
Hector, as an added revenge. Yet in spite of this dishonour
Apollo kept the body fresh and free from corruption, and
drove away the dogs that would have eaten it. At last the gods
became angry at this shameful treatment of a dead enemy, and
Hermes himself led old Priam, the Trojan king, to Achilles'
tent at night, bearing gifts, to try to ransom the body of his
son. Hermes cast a deep sleep on the sentries, so that Priam
with his attendant and the mule-cart laden with treasure
passed unnoticed through the body of the host.

Priam found Achilles seated in his tent, and going up to him
he clasped his knees in a gesture of supplication and kissed the
dreadful hands that had killed so many of his sons. Achilles
marvelled to see him, and Priam besought him: "Think of
your own father, godlike Achilles, who is an old man as I am.
Perhaps he too is helpless, at the mercy of his neighbours;

Mourning women

even so his son still lives, and he looks forward with rejoicing to his dear son's return from Troy. But I who had many sons now have lost almost all, and last the bravest, Hector, the strong tower of our city. On his account I have come to you, to offer a great ransom for his body. Remember your own father and show pity to me, who have done what no man ever yet forced himself to do, kissed the hands that slew my son."

Achilles wept at Priam's words, thinking now of his father Peleus and now of his friend Patroclus, and Priam at his feet wept for Hector, so that the tent was filled with lamentation.

At last Achilles raised Priam to his feet, saying, "Unhappy man, how could you have the courage to come alone to the ships as a suppliant to the slayer of your sons? Surely your heart must be of iron. But sit beside me, and we will hide our griefs in our hearts, for weeping cannot help us. This is the lot the gods have spun for miserable men, to live in pain; yet they themselves are sorrowless. So it is with my father Peleus, the hero, blessed in his marriage with a goddess: for he has no child but only me, who am fated to an early death; and I cannot stay with him in his age, since it is my destiny here at Troy to trouble you and your sons." Then Achilles called aloud on his dead friend Patroclus to forgive him for leaving his revenge unfinished; for he had meant to throw Hector's body to the dogs rather than let his family bury it. He took the gifts and gave Priam the body, and Priam returned with it to Troy, the Greeks holding back their forces from the city until the funeral rites were accomplished.

THE FALL OF THE CITY

Set where the upper streams of Simois flow
Was the Palladium, high 'mid rock and wood;
And Hector was in Ilium far below,
And fought, and saw it not – but there it stood!

It stood; and sun and moonshine rained their light
On the pure columns of its glen-built hall.
Backward and forward rolled the waves of fight
Round Troy; but while this stood, Troy could not fall.

MATTHEW ARNOLD

Not long after the death of Hector, Achilles too met his end. Hidden in a cloud, the archer-god Apollo met Paris in the thick of battle beside the Scaean Gate and guided his hand, so that his arrow struck Achilles in his vulnerable heel. His cousin Ajax carried his body through the host back to the Greek camp, while Odysseus fought off all who tried to stop him.

Funeral games were held in Achilles' honour, as for all the great heroes killed in the war. His mother Thetis offered his divinely-wrought armour as a prize to the most valiant of the Greeks left alive. Ajax and Odysseus both claimed this recognition, which the common vote adjudged to Odysseus. The mortified Ajax went into a mad battle-rage, striking out in the dark at harmless cattle that Athene, the friend of Odysseus, made him mistake for his enemies until his frenzy was exhausted. When in the morning he came to his senses and saw the havoc he had made, he threw himself on his sword.

Calchas the prophet now declared that Troy could not be taken without the help of Heracles' bow and arrows. These had been given many years before by the dying hero to Philoctetes, as a reward for his lighting the pyre on Mount Oeta; but Philoctetes had been left alone on an Aegean island because of his offensive wound. Odysseus and one companion now sailed back to find him. Philoctetes, whose distrust was soon overcome by their kind words and promises, returned with them to the Greek camp. Here a surgeon successfully treated the wound, and on his recovery Philoctetes went out to the field of battle and shot Paris mortally with the fatal bow. The Trojans carried their dying prince to Mount Ida, where he implored the help of his forsaken mistress Oenone, who was skilled in healing drugs. But she remembered his desertion of her, and refused, and he was borne back to Troy to die.

One more condition remained to be fulfilled before the city could fall. The Trojans guarded in a rich shrine an ancient and famous image of Pallas Athene, known as the Palladion, with which the city's fortunes were bound up. This Odysseus stole away, creeping under the cover of night.

After Philoctetes and his weapons had been fetched and the Palladion carried off, Athene put into the minds of the Greeks a plan whereby the city could be taken. They built an enormous horse of wooden planks, large enough to hold a small company of armed men in its belly, and carved on its flank a dedication to the goddess Athene. Leaving it on the shore, they broke up

Odysseus carrying off the Palladion

their camp, burned the more permanent structures in it, and took to their fleet and sailed out of sight. The Trojans, amazed and delighted to see them go, held earnest debate about the wooden horse. Some were for burning it where it stood, fearing a trap. Others, afraid of desecrating the goddess' property and hoping to win her to their side, counselled bringing it with all honour to the city. While they were still arguing, a portent occurred that settled the matter.

Foremost among those who suspected the horse was the priest Laocoön, who declared, "I mistrust the Greeks even when they bring gifts." Having done his best to persuade his fellow-citizens, he went down to the shore with his two sons to offer sacrifice to Poseidon. Apollo happened to see them go, and remembering that this man had once grievously offended him, he sent two monstrous serpents up out of the sea, which coiled about the father and the two boys and despite their struggles crushed them wretchedly to death. The Trojans interpreted this as a punishment from the gods for Laocoön's opposition to the horse, and were all the more determined to bring it into their city. The only one still to oppose it was Priam's daughter Cassandra, a priestess with the gift of prophecy, who could get nobody to listen to her tale of the griefs that would follow.

As the Trojans were preparing to drag the horse in, a lone Greek soldier, who had been left behind, appeared at the gates and begged Priam to give him shelter. His story was that Odysseus and some of the other Greek leaders had plotted against his life, so that he had escaped to Troy rather than go with them. Questioned about the horse, he replied eagerly that it had been built as an offering to Athene, who after having befriended the Greeks for so long was now angry with them for stealing her sacred image from its shrine in Troy. "But why then was the horse made so large?" "For fear that you should take it into the city and gain Athene's favour for your side." Nothing more was needed to convince the Trojans: they immediately laid down rollers over a carpet of flowers and dragged the horse in with shouts of rejoicing, though they had to break down part of the city wall to do so. They might not have been so hasty if they had known their guest to be Sinon, a cousin of the wily Odysseus.

When darkness fell and found the Trojans celebrating their enemies' departure with feasting and drinking, the Greek fleet, which had merely rounded the nearest cape, turned rapidly back towards Troy. Tired from their revelling, the Trojans were all in a deep sleep when thirty armed men, Odysseus among them, slipped down a rope-ladder from the belly of the horse and signalled to their comrades outside the walls. The whole Greek army was soon crowding the streets and ransacking the houses, slaughtering their unarmed defenders.

Priam died on the palace steps, the last of his sons falling around him, and his body was cast unburied on the tomb of Achilles. His queen Hecabe, with Hector's widow Andromache and other high-born Trojan women, was led off into captivity. Hector's little son was thrown from the battlements, for fear he should avenge his city when he grew to be a man. The wronged Menelaus went straight to the apartment of Helen, intending to avenge on her all the sorrows of the long war; but her god-born beauty still shone in her worn face, and his heart relenting, he cast away his sword and led her gently to the ships.

Having massacred its betrayed defenders, the Greeks sacked and burned the city, dividing up as plunder everything they could carry away with them, both goods and captives.

THE RETURNS: MENELAUS

> *Dear is the memory of our wedded lives,*
> *And dear the last embraces of our wives*
> *And their warm tears: but all hath suffer'd change:*
> *For surely now our household hearths are cold,*
> *Our sons inherit us: our looks are strange:*
> *And we should come like ghosts to trouble joy.*
> *Or else the island princes over-bold*
> *Have eat our substance, and the minstrel sings*
> *Before them of the ten years' war in Troy,*
> *And our great deeds, as half-forgotten things.*

> TENNYSON

The victorious Greeks looted and destroyed without restraint; and their ferocity brought on them retribution from the gods, especially from Athene. On the night of Troy's fall the prophetess Cassandra took refuge in Athene's temple, where the Greeks who broke in found her clinging to a wooden statue that now replaced the Palladion. By dragging her forcibly away, they flouted Athene's protection and violated her sanctuary. The man chiefly responsible for this was one Ajax – not the great Ajax, who died before the war ended, but a lesser man. The injured goddess persuaded Poseidon to help her take vengeance, by stirring up the seas and snatching from many their hope of return. Thus two powerful divinities who

Athene and Poseidon

had been on the side of the Greeks now became their bitter enemies.

Poseidon himself took care of the lesser Ajax, wrecking his ship on a rocky shore. Ajax would have escaped with a wetting if he had not boasted as he scrambled up the rocks that the gods couldn't drown him if they tried: the angry Poseidon split the rock Ajax stood on with his trident and made him a liar.

The first to suffer from Athene's wrath was Menelaus, who lost most of his fleet in a violent storm. Then he was held up with the remaining five ships in Egypt, waiting for favourable winds. Just as his men were running out of provisions and had taken to fishing with improvised tackle, a sea-nymph, taking pity on Menelaus, came up to him as he was sitting by himself and advised him to seek out her father Proteus, an old immortal living under the sea off the Egyptian coast. He, if Menelaus could only hold him fast, would advise him about his journey. Giving him precise instructions as to how Proteus could be captured, she then dived back under the sea.

Menelaus set off for the island of Pharos, three of his men with him, and there on the shore they lay in wait under four fresh sealskins provided by the nymph, who gave them also some divine ambrosia to ward off the stench. For a long morning they watched while the seals came up to bask on the shore, until at noon up came the old man of the sea himself, who counted over the seals like a shepherd his flock before lying down to sleep in the midst of them. Then the four rushed on him with a shout and seized him; whereupon he began to change his shape, becoming a lion, a dragon, all manner of wild beasts, then running water, then a tree; but Menelaus and the sailors still held fast. At last Proteus gave in, admitting that he recognized Menelaus and knew why he had come. He advised Menelaus if he wanted to break the calm, to return to Egypt and offer generous sacrifices to Zeus and the other gods, who would then let him finish his voyage.

When Menelaus asked Proteus how his friends were faring on their way home, the old prophet had many sad tales to tell him, of shipwreck on the sea and forgetfulness or worse at home. He ended by telling Menelaus of his own further fate. "You shall not die in Sparta, but the gods will take you to the Elysian fields at the world's end. There life is pleasanter than anywhere else, for there falls no rain, nor hail, nor snow, but always a fresh singing breeze blows from the sea and renews the spirits of men. You shall enter this happy place because you are married to fair Helen and thus are the son-in-law of Zeus." Then he slipped back into the sea, and Menelaus with a heavy heart returned to the ships on the Egyptian shore, arriving not long afterwards with Helen at his palace in Sparta.

THE RETURNS: AGAMEMNON

> *Sometime let gorgeous Tragedy*
> *In sceptr'd pall come sweeping by,*
> *Presenting Thebes', or Pelops' line.*
> MILTON

For Menelaus' brother Agamemnon a worse fate was reserved. Unlike so many of the others, he reached his palace in Mycenae with very little trouble, bringing with him as part of his spoils Priam's daughter, the prophetess Cassandra. He was royally welcomed home by his queen Clytemnestra, the sister of Helen, who spread a feast for him and first of all led him to the bath to wash off the dust of his travels. As he stepped out of the bath, she held out a robe; but instead of helping him into it, she threw it over his head, so that he could not stir. Then she and Agamemnon's cousin Aegisthus, with whom she had been plotting during the long years of the war, stabbed him to death. Cassandra, who knew already what was to happen, fell next by Clytemnestra's hand.

This was only one in a long series of crimes committed in that ill-fated family. For Agamemnon's great-grandfather was Tantalus, who feasted at the tables of the gods as their friend until he offended them by betraying their confidence and by a still worse outrage: once when they were paying him a return visit, he killed and served up to them in a stew his young son Pelops, to test their powers of detection. They all rose in horror from the board, excepting Demeter, who, still grieving for her daughter, had eaten some flesh from the shoulder without noticing what it was she ate. First the gods tumbled Tantalus down to the underworld, where he is condemned to stand forever thirsting in a stream that flees when he tries to drink of it, and hungering under a fruit-tree that continually snatches its laden branches away from him. Then they assembled the pieces of Pelops out of the stew-pot and brought him back to life, replacing the missing shoulder with one made of ivory.

Pelops' two sons, Atreus and Thyestes, quarrelled over the throne of Mycenae, which by the expressed will of Zeus fell to Atreus. Discovering meanwhile that Thyestes had insulted his young bride, Atreus sent him a friendly invitation to come and share the city with him, and spread a banquet before him in welcome. When Thyestes had eaten heartily, Atreus made a servant carry in to him on a dish all that was left of the bloody banquet, the remains of Thyestes' murdered sons. Thyestes rose from the table, choking on the unnatural meat, and before he left Mycenae he turned and pronounced a curse on the house of Atreus.

Both these warring brothers had sons who reached manhood. The revengeful Atreus was the father of Agamemnon and Menelaus, who married sisters, the Spartan princesses Clytemnestra and Helen; two unlucky marriages. Menelaus escaped the worst effects of the curse, but Agamemnon felt its full force in his death. Thyestes' surviving son Aegisthus murdered his uncle Atreus, and lived to assist Agamemnon's wife in his destruction. Agamemnon was murdered in revenge not only for his father's crime but also for his consenting to the sacrifice of his daughter Iphigeneia.

Such a chain of horrors could not go unnoticed by the gods, who at last intervened. Apollo with Zeus' consent encouraged Agamemnon's son Orestes, now grown to manhood, to avenge his father's death by the murder of his mother Clytemnestra and her guilty friend. This Orestes carried out, with the willing help of his sister Electra.

The act brought on Orestes the hatred of the Erinyes, the three horrible hags who smell out the blood of those who die by the hand of their kin and demand punishment: they are so ancient that they despise the Olympian gods as newcomers and upstarts. The Erinyes pursued Orestes over land and sea, driving him to madness and delusion. After a year of exile he came to Athens, with the avengers still on his heels. They dragged him before the Areopagus, the Athenian court of judgement. Here the Erinyes were his chief accusers, while Apollo himself came forward in his defence. The question at issue was whether his father's murder justified a son in killing his mother. Apollo in his speech declared that the mother who bore a child was not so essentially his parent as the father. The twelve judges then cast their votes, which were found to be evenly divided; so Athene as the city's patron goddess was called upon to decide. Athene, who not only never became a wife or mother herself but moreover was born from the head of Zeus, took an anti-feminist view. "I am for the father," she announced, giving judgement in Orestes' favour. This done, she pacified the Erinyes, who, baulked of their victim, were gnashing their long tusks. She promised them a gloomy shrine under the Athenian Acropolis, where henceforward they should receive offerings and perpetual worship under the new name of the "Eumenides" – no longer the Furies but the Kindly Ones.

THE RETURNS: AENEAS

Golden branch amid the shadows,
kings and realms that pass to rise no more.

TENNYSON

Another story of the aftermath of Troy, though not exactly a "return", is that of the wanderings of one of the Trojan princes, Aeneas, the son of the goddess Aphrodite and a mortal man, Anchises, with whom she fell in love while he was tending his flock on the slopes of Mount Ida. Her passion for him was sent by Zeus, in revenge for the many humiliations that she and her prankish son Eros had inflicted on him and the other gods. Anchises later was so foolish as to boast of his remarkable conquest, and Zeus, seeing that the joke was getting out of hand, loosed a thunderbolt at him. Aphrodite interposed her marvellous girdle and saved his life, but he was never able to walk again.

Protected by his divine mother, Aeneas escaped from the flames of Troy, bearing his old father on his back and the figures of his household gods in his arms, accompanied by a few friends and his little son Ascanius. He had been told in a dream that it was his destiny to found a nation in a country lying far to the west, Italy, to which divine guidance would eventually bring them. A prophet advised them how to direct their journey: they must take a roundabout way in order to avoid certain perils they would not be strong enough to overcome. Many years of wandering lay before them, at the end of which they would reach their new home.

Passing Sicily, where lived the monster Polyphemus, who shouted terrible threats after them from the shore, they were met by a fearful storm, sent by Hera, who hated all the Trojans but especially Aeneas, and had resolved that he should never reach Italy. He with his small fleet came safely through the storm, however, and landed near the city of Carthage in North Africa. Carthage was under the protection of Hera, who knew that the city the Trojans were destined to found would in later times go to war against Carthage, raze it to the ground, and lay waste all the surrounding territory; so she devised a plan to divert Aeneas from his course. The hero was to fall in love with Dido, the beautiful early-widowed Carthaginian queen, and settle quietly down as her consort. His mother Aphrodite was willing to help entangle Aeneas in this love-affair, knowing what Hera did not know, that Zeus had sworn her son should fulfil his destiny and become the founder of the greatest empire on earth.

For a time Aeneas lived at Carthage, happy in Dido's love. But when he and his men were thoroughly rested and refreshed from the long campaign at Troy and their wanderings since, the gods decided to end this trifling. Hermes, sent from Zeus, arrived one day to remind Aeneas of his duty. Ashamed of his luxurious idleness, Aeneas immediately ordered his men to prepare for departure, heedless of Dido's pleading and laments. That very night the ships set sail, and that same night Dido had raised a high funeral pyre, on which she stabbed herself to death, calling on the gods to avenge her fate. From this harsh return for her generosity is supposed to have sprung the enmity between Carthage and the race of Aeneas, later the Roman people.

Leaving Carthage behind, Aeneas held his course towards Italy. The fleet had again left Sicily behind when he lost his valued and experienced pilot, Palinurus, who one night fell asleep at the helm and slid into the sea. Aeneas, awake while his men slept, saw that the ship had lost its pilot and was drifting. He took the helm himself and guided the ship all that night, grieving for his friend: "Alas, Palinurus, you trusted too much in the sky and the quiet sea: now you will lie unburied on an unknown shore."

Passing the Sirens' rock, Aeneas landed on the west coast of Italy. There he sought out the Sibyl of Cumae, the prophetic priestess of Apollo, to enquire the will of the gods about his journey. She gave him no advice herself, but promised to guide him to the underworld where he could consult the ghost of his old father Anchises, who had died on the way in Sicily. The path to the lower world was hard and dangerous, and to undertake it in safety Aeneas must carry in his hand the mysterious golden bough, sacred to Persephone, the queen of the dead. Guided by two doves sent by his mother, Aeneas saw the golden bough glimmering in the dark grove surrounding Lake Avernus, where the underworld pathway began, and breaking it off he carried it back to the Sibyl. She, after sacrificing to Hecate, led him in the night down the steep road to Tartarus.

> *Four infernal rivers, that disgorge*
> *Into the burning lake their baleful streams –*
> *Abhorrèd Styx, the flood of deadly hate;*
> *Sad Acheron of sorrow, black and deep;*
> *Cocytus, named of lamentation loud*
> *Heard on the rueful stream; fierce Phlegethon,*
> *Whose waves of torrent fire inflame with rage.*
> *Far off from these, a slow and silent stream,*
> *Lethe, the river of oblivion, rolls*
> *Her wat'ry labyrinth, whereof who drinks*
> *Forthwith his former state and being forgets,*
> *Forgets both joy and grief, pleasure and pain.*
>   **MILTON**

Five rivers encircle and wind through the abode of the dead: Styx or the Hateful, the river by which Zeus swears, Acheron the Sorrowful, Phlegethon the Fiery, Cocytus or Lamentation, and Lethe, the river of Forgetfulness. Their banks are crowded with pitiful wailing souls, waiting for Charon the infernal ferryman to row them over in his creaky boat. The golden bough was sufficient passport for Aeneas and his guide, who quickly reached the farther shore, where they placated the three-headed watchdog Cerberus by throwing him small cakes brought for the purpose. Among the fields of the dead they met the pale shade of Dido, who passed them without a look or word, pale with anger and bleeding from her mortal wound. At last they found Anchises, who greeted his son affectionately, instructed him where he should settle and how he should proceed, and prophesied to him the future glory of Rome.

Back on the Italian shore, Aeneas with his men made his way to Latium, the district around the mouth of the Tiber where Rome was eventually to be founded. There Hera stirred up trouble for them among the inhabitants. Coming in peace and asking only for a place to settle, they met armed resistance and had to make war for the right to stay. At length Aeneas put down all his enemies, and he married Lavinia, the daughter of Latinus the friendly king of Latium; and from them sprang the Roman people.

THE RETURN OF ODYSSEUS

> *That long wand'ring Greek*
> *That for his love refusèd deity.*
>
> SPENSER

The longest tale of wanderings on the return from Troy is that of Odysseus, the wily king of the rocky island of Ithaca in the

Ionian Sea, who after the ten-years' siege took ten years more to get home. One of the first places where his fleet put in was the land of the Lotus-Eaters, gentle people whose main food was the lotus-fruit, which they offered to the sailors. Those who ate immediately forgot about the long war behind them and their homes ahead, and thought of nothing but staying here contentedly forever. Odysseus needed all his presence of mind to contend with this peril: he had the men carried back on board immediately, and kept them tied up until the effect wore off.

Next they came to the island of Sicily, inhabited by the dangerous Cyclopes, giants with a single eye in the middle of their foreheads. They lived as shepherds, sleeping with their flocks in solitary caves among the rocks. Odysseus and some of his men entered one of these caves during the day while its owner Polyphemus was out. They knew it belonged to someone, as there were kids and lambs penned at the back and around the walls were bowls, milk-pails and newly-made cheeses. The Greeks made themselves comfortable, lighting a fire and helping themselves to the goat's-milk cheeses. In the evening Polyphemus came home, drove his flock into the cave, and afterwards blocked the entrance with a huge stone. Then he caught sight of the travellers, who politely requested his hospitality, Odysseus acting as spokesman. The answer they received was a rough one: "Stranger, you are a fool, or you don't know where you are. Why talk about Zeus and his protection of suppliants? We Cyclopes are stronger than he is, and care nothing for his laws." So saying, he snatched up two of Odysseus' comrades, dashed their brains out on the cavern floor, and gobbled them down for his evening meal. The others watched horror-struck as he swilled down the last morsels with milk and then stretched himself out on the ground to sleep. Odysseus thought of killing him with his sword, but what good would that have done them? they could never have moved away the stone from the cavern's mouth.

After a night passed in fear and lamentation, they watched the monster dispose of two more men for his breakfast; then having milked the she-goats he shoved away the stone and drove out his flock, blocking the cave mouth again immediately. In his absence, they worked out a plan. At night, after Polyphemus had again supped off two of their fellows, Odysseus approached him with a bowlful of some wine he had with him, pretending that he hoped with this offering to soften the giant's heart. Polyphemus greedily gulped it down and demanded more. After three bowlfuls, he asked Odysseus' name and promised to give him a present. "My name is Oudeis (No one): now what will you give me?" "Oudeis shall be eaten last of his companions: that is his present;" and with that the Cyclops fell into a drunken sleep. Immediately Odysseus jumped up and seized a huge pole of fresh-cut olive-wood that was lying in the cave, and when he had sharpened one end, the men thrust it into the embers of the fire to heat. When the sap began to hiss and run out, they drew it from the fire and thrust the point into the Cyclops' single eye as he lay sleeping with his head flung back. Polyphemus screamed till the cave re-echoed, and staggered to his feet blinded and bellowing. The other Cyclopes living near by came running to find out the cause of the disturbance; but when they heard Polyphemus roaring, "No one has blinded me! No one is murdering me!" they went grumbling back to their caves to finish their night's sleep.

While the giant groaned and stumbled about the cave, Odysseus was thinking up a stratagem whereby he and his men might escape. He noiselessly seized the rams of the flock and bound them together in threes, strapping a man under each of the middle ones. For himself he took the largest of all the rams, clinging to the thick wool under the belly. When morning came, Polyphemus let out his flock, passing his hand over each of the animals' backs as they went by but missing the men underneath. When Odysseus' own ram had got safely outside he let go and ran to untie all the others. Reaching their ships and silencing their friends' cries of wonderment and welcome, they took their places at the oars and began to row away. Then Odysseus stood up and shouted back at Polyphemus: "You brute, would you eat up harmless travellers? The gods did well to punish you for such wickedness." Polyphemus in a rage threw half a mountain at them, so violently that they were driven back towards the shore. When by hard rowing they were once more well out to sea, Odysseus began to taunt him again, though his companions begged him not to: "If anyone asks who spoiled that handsome eye of yours, tell him it was Odysseus of Ithaca who did it." Then the Cyclops lifted up his hands to heaven and prayed to his father Poseidon. "Hear me, great god of the sea: if I am indeed your son, see to it that Odysseus never gets home alive, or if he does, may he suffer the loss of his ships, his men and all he has, and return friendless and destitute to a troubled house." Poseidon heard his prayer, and the Greeks rowed on sorrowful for their friends and fearful of what was to come.

They came next to the floating island of Aeolus the god of the winds, where he lived with his six sons who were married to their six sisters. There they were kindly entertained, and when Odysseus left, Aeolus gave him as a parting present a skin bag in which were shut up all the winds unfavourable to the homeward journey – all of them, that is, but the west wind which helped them along. For nine days and nine nights they sped forward, until on the tenth they could make out their homeland rising out of the sea, and see the fires burning the autumn stubble. Then Odysseus, weary with watching, fell into a light sleep. His men began to talk among themselves, saying that he was bringing home treasure in that sack, and that they who had shared his troubles and labours should have a share in his rewards as well. One of them untied the cord round the mouth; whereupon all the winds burst out howling together in a storm that carried ships and weeping men far from their native land. Driven back to the Aeolian island, Odysseus entered the god's house and sat down by the hearth as a suppliant, explaining the misfortune that had brought him back and asking a second time for help. For all that he could say, the god was angry at the misuse of his gift and declared that a man so unlucky must be one deservedly hated by heaven. Odysseus sadly returned to the ships, having gained nothing by his visit, and they set off once more.

After long rowing, they arrived at the country where lived the Laestrygonians, man-eating giants, who waited till most of the fleet had moored in their land-locked harbour and then began to cast huge rocks down on the ships and spear the men like fish. All caught within the harbour died a cruel death, while Odysseus, who had prudently made fast his own ship just outside, cut the cable with his sword and shouted to the men to row for their lives. So they sailed on, glad to have escaped death but sorrowful for the loss of their friends.

> *Who knows not Circe,*
> *The daughter of the Sun, whose charmèd cup*
> *Whoever tasted lost his upright shape,*
> *And downward fell into a grovelling swine?*
>
> MILTON

In time they came to the island of Aiaia, the home of the great and cunning goddess Circe, sister to the magician Aietes and child of the Sun. There they beached their ship in a safe harbour, and for two days and nights they lay on the shore, worn out with their troubles. On the third day Odysseus, having no idea of their whereabouts, sent off some of his men under his lieutenant Eurylochus in the direction where he had seen the smoke of a house rising among the trees.

As the band approached the house, they were met by all
kinds of wild beasts, wolves and mountain lions among them,
which to their amazement were not fierce at all but fawned on
them like dogs on their master. Standing at the house gates,
they could hear the goddess working at her loom within, and
all the house rang with her singing. As soon as they called to
her, she opened the gates and invited them in with kind words,

Circe

setting food and wine before them – all but the cautious
Eurylochus, who stayed mistrustfully outside. And the event
proved him right, for the moment the men had swallowed
Circe's drugged wine, she touched them on the shoulder with
her wand and they were transformed into pigs, hairy and
grunting, and shut up in her pigsties. Then, too late, they
understood the nature of the strange animals in the wood.

When his comrades failed to return, Eurylochus hastened
back in terror and distress to Odysseus, who immediately set
out to find them. In the enchanted grove surrounding the
house he met the god Hermes, in the likeness of a young man,

recognizable by the golden herald's staff he always carried. Hermes greeted Odysseus kindly, explained the fate of his companions, and gave him a magical herb called moly that would protect him against Circe's enchantments. The root of moly is black, it has a milk-white flower, and only the gods can uproot it from the earth.

Welcomed by Circe, Odysseus drank her wine without becoming stupefied by it; and when she struck him with her wand, crying, "Be off to the pigsty with your friends!", he rushed at her with his sword and made her fall at his feet in supplication. "Who are you, that you can withstand my enchantments? You can only be Odysseus, who was destined to come here: put up your sword and let us be friends." Odysseus relented only after she had promised to release not only his comrades but all her other captives as well. Thereafter she entertained them all so royally that they stayed with her for a whole year without once thinking of their homes.

At length Odysseus' men began to press him to continue the journey, and he asked the goddess for her advice. "Before you can reach your homeland, you must go to the house of Hades and his queen Persephone to consult the ghost of Teiresias, the blind prophet of Thebes. He alone of all the dead preserves his understanding, while the other ghosts flit mindlessly about. Enter your ship, set the sails, and the wind will carry you straight to the shore of Persephone's country, where the sun never shines, where black poplars stand in groves and the willows drop their fruit before it ripens. Where the rivers Phlegethon and Cocytus flow into Acheron, there you must dig a trench and pour a drink-offering to the dead. Then sacrifice a ram and a black ewe with your face turned away, and let their blood run into the trench. The ghosts of the dead will crowd about it and try to drink, but you must keep them off with your sword until Teiresias has drunk of the blood and answered all your questions. He will direct you over the sea and tell you how you will reach home."

All happened as the goddess had promised. When Odysseus poured out the blood of the sheep, the ghosts came trooping up from the ground, eager to drink it, flitting with faint screams around the trench. Odysseus held them all back till the shade of Teiresias had lapped its fill and gathered strength enough to speak. "You will have a hard journey home, pursued by the anger of Poseidon; but you may still get there if you can keep your men when they get to Sicily from driving off the oxen of the Sun, who hears and sees everything. Even then, you are destined to lose all your men and to arrive in wretchedness in another man's ship: then you will find trouble in your house, strangers devouring your property and humiliating your patient wife Penelope. You will get rid of them, but then you must undertake another journey to placate Poseidon, carrying an oar over your shoulder until you reach a land where men do not salt their food, have never heard of the sea, and mistake the oar for a winnowing-fan. There you will set up the oar in the ground and sacrifice to Poseidon; afterwards you may go home and live to a quiet old age, but death shall come to you from the sea at last."

Teiresias then told Odysseus that if he wished to speak with any more of the ghosts, particularly that of his mother, he should let them drink of the blood, and then their memory and speech would return. Odysseus' mother confirmed Teiresias' words about the trouble in Ithaca, telling him how the chief men of the town, supposing him dead, had moved into his house under pretext of courting his wife, while his old father was reduced to poverty and his son Telemachus, now a grown man, was running the estate as best he could.

When she had finished speaking, Odysseus tried to embrace his mother; but though he stretched out his arms to her three times, each time she flitted from him like a phantom or a dream. At last he cried out, "Does Persephone want to torment

me, troubled as I am, by mocking me with an empty shadow?"
"My son," she replied, "most unfortunate of men, it is not that
Persephone deludes you, but we are all like this when we are
dead. Our sinews no longer hold our flesh and bones together,
and nothing is left but a fleeting ghost."

Lastly there came to the trench the shades of some of
Odysseus' companions in the war. Among them was Achilles,
who asked him weeping, "Why have you ventured to this
miserable realm, among the empty ghosts of the dead?"
Odysseus tried to cheer him, saying: "Surely you should be
contented. No man was ever blessed as you have been, for
living you were honoured among us like the gods, and now you
lord it mightily among the dead. Is that so evil a fate?" "Do
not try to praise death to me," Achilles replied. "I would
rather serve as a bondman to a poor farmer, if only I might be
above the earth, than be king of kings over all the host of the
dead."

> *And the Sirens, taught to kill*
> *With their sweet voice,*
> *Make every echoing rock reply*
> *Unto their gentle murmuring noise.*
>
> THOMAS CAMPION

Leaving the dark grove of Persephone, Odysseus resumed
the homeward voyage. Now they approached the island of
the Sirens, the fatal singers who sit in a green meadow heaped
with the rotting bones of those they have decoyed. Circe had
warned him of them, advising him to stop his men's ears with
wax, which he did; but he left his own ears free, having himself
bound to the mast instead so that he could not leap out to
destruction. Next they had to pass between the rock of the
six-headed yelping monster Scylla and the terrible whirlpool
Charybdis; by keeping to Scylla's side of the channel they got

by without being sucked down, but they paid for their escape: as they passed, each of her six heads scooped up one man.

Circe as well as Teiresias had warned Odysseus about the herds of the Sun on the island of Sicily, and the peril attendant on the theft of a single beast. He was very careful to warn his men that they must content themselves while there with the

Odysseus and the Sirens

food Circe had sent along in the ship. At first his counsels prevailed. But the anger of the gods still pursued them: first Zeus sent a storm, and then a contrary wind blew steadily for a month, so that they exhausted their provisions and still could not leave the island. At last they took to fishing and setting traps for small birds, with no luck at all. Then one day when Odysseus was sleeping a little way off, his lieutenant Eurylochus gathered the others around him and declared they would starve if they went on obeying the order. Hunger overcame prudence, and Odysseus when he returned to the ship smelt roast beef and cursed his fate. The Sun in a rage went to Zeus and swore he would go down to the house of

Hades and shine among the dead if the loss of his beloved
cattle was not made up to him. Zeus could appease him only by
promising to shatter the ship into little bits with a thunderbolt.
Portents of disaster began immediately: the hides of the dead
cattle crawled about, and the meat as it was being roasted and
eaten lowed like living cows.

When at last the wind dropped, the ship put out to sea.
Immediately the sky darkened, a terrific squall blew up, and
Zeus let fly with his thunderbolts. The ship went whirling
round and round: all the men were swept from the decks and
were either drowned or struck by the lightning. Odysseus
managed to hang on to some pieces of wreckage from which
he improvised a raft, and being carried along all night by the
waves, in the morning he found himself back on the brink of
Charybdis. He only just escaped alive, by clinging to a solitary
tree growing on a rock until his raft, sucked in by the whirlpool,
was disgorged again.

Eventually the raft brought him to the island of Ogygia,
where the nymph Calypso received him kindly, promising him
eternal youth like her own if he would only stay with her. She
was in a position to enforce her wishes, as Odysseus for all his
longing for home had no means of getting away. At last after
seven years Athene, concerned for the troubles of his wife
and son as well as his own, persuaded Zeus to send Hermes
to Calypso with a message that she had kept Odysseus long
enough and must let him go. Calypso was angry, but could not
move the gods; so she went to Odysseus where he was sitting
homesick on the beach looking at the sea, and told him that if
he persisted in his preference for a troubled house and a wife
neither immortal nor divinely beautiful, she would help him
to build and equip a raft strong enough to take him home.
Wondering at her willingness, he set gladly to work. In five
days the raft was completed and fully stocked with provisions,
and Odysseus set out on it, keeping the Bear on his left as

Calypso had instructed him, and guiding his raft with a rudder. He had almost reached the land of the Phaeacians when Poseidon caught sight of him sailing along and flew into a rage. "The gods have been favouring this fellow: well, they forgot about me." He blew up the worst storm he could muster, commanding the winds of all the four quarters to fall upon Odysseus and his makeshift vessel, sweeping him into the roaring water and snatching the raft out of his grasp. Just as Odysseus was giving up hope, the sea-goddess Ino appeared and lent him her veil, which held him up until after great efforts he was able to reach the shore. There he struggled into the mouth of a river and scrambled up on the bank, casting the veil back into the water. He lay there until morning, worn out with his troubles.

When dawn broke, Nausicaa, the beautiful daughter of King Alcinoüs and Queen Arete, came down to the river-mouth with her women to do the palace washing. After it was done and the linen folded to be carried back in the wagon, the princess threw a ball to one of the girls, who missed it, letting it drop into the water. Their cry awoke the hero, who came out from the bushes that had sheltered him and walked forward, naked, wild-eyed with hunger, and bruised from his struggle with the sea. Nausicaa, moved by his evident distress, had him bathed and clothed and brought him back to the town; but being a princess of remarkable discretion, she left it to him to present himself at the palace. "So that no scandal will be caused by my taking a strange man under my protection, you must wait at the outskirts of the town to allow us to get home, before you ask your way to the house of my father Alcinoüs. When you come into the building, walk straight through the inner court till you come to my mother Arete, sitting by the fire and spinning her purple wool with her maids around her. Close to her sits my father, drinking like the immortal gods; but pay no attention to him, go up to my mother and lay your hands on her knees in supplication if you want to see your home again."

Guided by Athene, Odysseus reached the palace, splendid like the sun or the moon and surrounded by a walled garden in which grew every kind of fruit-tree, whose fruit never failed the whole year round, a new crop ripening as the old was gathered. On either side of the gateway sat dogs of gold and silver, made by Hephaestus to guard the house, ageless and deathless for ever: within were golden statues with torches in their hands, to light the banqueters by night.

Entering, Odysseus went straight to Queen Arete as he had been told. All went well and he was kindly welcomed. Alcinoüs summoned the chief citizens of Phaeacia to a feast, where they were entertained by the bard Demodocus, whom the Muse dearly loved but rewarded with both good and evil, bringing him the divine gift of song but taking away his sight. Demodocus began to sing of the events at Troy, whereupon Odysseus, who was still unknown to the court, drew his cloak over his face and wept. Alcinoüs, noting his grief, began to suspect who his guest was, and he questioned him until Odysseus consented to tell the whole story of his travels.

Afterwards Alcinoüs sent off Odysseus loaded with gifts in one of the intelligent ships of the Phaeacians, that know where they are going without rudder or pilot. Then was fulfilled an old prophecy: Poseidon, from whom were descended both Alcinoüs and his wife Arete, had always threatened that one day, if the Phaeacians continued to send escorts with everyone who asked for them, he would wreck one of their ships on its way home from such a mission and bury their city under a high mountain. When Poseidon saw the Phaeacian ship reach Ithaca and Odysseus set ashore by the sailors, he was angry, and waiting till the ship had almost reached home, he struck it with the flat of his hand just off-shore, turning it into a rock. Then Alcinoüs, remembering the prophecy, hastened with all the people to sacrifice to Poseidon, for fear he should carry out his threat and bury their city under a mountain; and there the story leaves them.

> *Homer doth tell in his abundant verse*
> *The long laborious travels of the man,*
> *And of his lady too he doth rehearse*
> *How she eludes with all the art she can*
> *The ungrateful love which other lords began;*
> *For of her lord false fame long since had sworn*
> *That Neptune's monsters had his carcass torn.*
> SIR JOHN DAVIES

Odysseus arriving on his native shore was greeted by Athene, who warned him of the dangers he must face at home, gave him the appearance of an old and wretched man, and brought him secretly to the hut of Eumaeus, his old swineherd. During his twenty years' absence, a group of princes from Ithaca and the neighbouring islands had been demanding the hand of his faithful wife Penelope, and with it the kingdom. She put them off by all the shifts she could, trusting in Odysseus' eventual return; and when at last she was compelled to name a day when she would choose among them, she promised to do it when she had finished the work she had at that moment on the loom – a shroud for her old father-in-law. The shroud was never finished, however, for she secretly unravelled every night almost as much as she had woven in the day. Meanwhile the unruly suitors had moved into the palace and were feasting themselves liberally on Odysseus' flocks, herds and store of wine. Their insolence and impatience increased daily, especially since just before this time one of Penelope's maids had told them why the web was taking so long. Penelope was now living all but imprisoned in the upper rooms, while her son Telemachus had travelled to Sparta to ask if Menelaus had any news of Odysseus.

Now that Odysseus had returned, Athene fetched Telemachus back from Sparta and brought him to Eumaeus' hut, where father and son greeted each other affectionately. Then they laid their plans to get rid of the troublesome suitors.

The next morning Telemachus went home to the palace, Odysseus coming after dressed as a poor old beggar. As he reached the gate his old hound Argus, lying in the path, recognized him and feebly wagged his tail. Odysseus dared not bend down and caress him, and as he walked away the old dog died.

When Odysseus appeared as a beggar in the hall, the suitors mocked at him and ill-treated him, one of them throwing a footstool that bruised his shoulder. Penelope, hearing of this, was angry, and sent for the beggar to ask if he knew anything of Odysseus. Coming into her presence, he told a long tale of having met her husband and heartened her with promises that he would soon be home; and all the time he spoke Penelope looked at her husband but did not know him. Odysseus pitied her and longed to reveal himself, but he was afraid she might accidentally betray him before his revenge was accomplished.

When she had heard the story, Penelope called an old servant, Eurycleia, who had been Odysseus' nurse, to come and bathe her guest's feet. No sooner did she bend over the tub than she recognized an old scar on his thigh that he had got hunting on Mount Parnassus many years ago with his grandfather Autolycus, the famous thief and liar. In her shock she dropped his foot so that the tub overturned, spilling the water out: immediately Odysseus caught her by the throat and commanded her to hold her tongue. "Child," she said, "what are you thinking of? You know that nothing can bend or break me: I will be as dumb as a stone or a lump of iron."

When Odysseus took leave of Penelope, who had noticed nothing, she told him that after all she feared her husband might be dead, that she was afraid to hold off the suitors any longer and was considering some trial of strength or skill by

which she might make her choice. Yet still she hesitated: she
had lately dreamed of a great eagle that descended from the
sky and destroyed a flock of geese as they fed at the trough:
might not this be an omen that Odysseus would return and
destroy the unwelcome suitors? "Stranger, I do not know what
to think. There are two gates through which dreams come to
us from the underworld, one of horn and one of ivory. Those
that come by the gate of ivory are empty and vain, but true
dreams pass the gate of horn: for my son's sake and my own,
I trust my dream was one of those." So saying, she went
upstairs to her couch, where Athene shed sweet sleep on her
eyes.

When day came, the suitors all arrived at the house and
began their usual feasting, heaping insults on Odysseus, who
held his peace. After they had eaten, Penelope brought down
from the store-room a great bow, with its quiver of arrows,
left behind twenty years ago by Odysseus when he went to the
war. She stood before the suitors and told them that she would
marry whichever one of them could string Odysseus' bow and
with it shoot an arrow through a series of twelve iron rings
set up in a row. All the suitors tried in turn to string the bow;
while they were trying, Odysseus went out to the courtyard
and made himself known to two old servants of whose fidelity
he was sure, the swineherd Eumaeus who had sheltered him
unknowing and another herdsman. These he directed to close
off the door to the women's apartment and the other exits of
the house. When he went back into the hall, the last of the
suitors had just given up. Odysseus asked if he might try, to
see what strength remained to him in his old age; the others
were angry, but Telemachus rebuked them and had it passed
to where he sat. After examining it a moment, Odysseus strung
it as easily as a bard fits a new string to his lyre, and shot an
arrow straight through the line of rings that had been set up.
Then he threw off his rags, signalled to Telemachus, who

sprang armed to his side, and began to shoot his quiverful of arrows at the suitors, who, helpless with amazement, fell one by one. When his arrows ran out, Eumaeus and the herdsman, who had provided themselves with armour from the store-room, came to his aid, and the goddess Athene stood by and encouraged them in the slaughter. Finally only two were left, wretches who had been compelled by the suitors to serve them, a priest who performed their sacrifices and a bard who sang for their entertainment. The priest begged for his life, but Odysseus would not hear him. "Many a time have you prayed to the gods to delay my homecoming," he said, and struck off the man's head as he knelt. Then the bard came forward: "You will be sorry if you kill a bard like me who can sing before both gods and men." Him Odysseus spared.

When at last Odysseus paused and looked about him, the hall was crowded with dead men, lying like fish hauled out of the sea and left on the bank to gasp their lives away. Then he opened the door of the women's apartment and called down the old nurse Eurycleia. When she saw that sight, she opened her mouth to cry out in triumph; but Odysseus checked her, saying, "Rejoice in silence: it is an unholy thing to triumph in the death of men. The anger of the gods and their own evil deeds have destroyed them." Under his direction the maids set to work thoroughly to cleanse the hall; meanwhile Eurycleia went upstairs with the light step of a young woman to tell Penelope that her husband had come home and made an end of the insolent suitors who had troubled his house. Penelope at first would not believe it, supposing her old servant to have gone mad. "Odysseus has met his death far from Ithaca," she said, "he will never return to his homeland." But she was persuaded at least to go down and see for herself.

Coming down into the hall, she seated herself by the fire opposite Odysseus and looked at him for a long time without speaking, so long that Telemachus began to reproach her

Hermes

with hard-heartedness. Still full of amazement, she would not believe until Odysseus had spoken to her of things that only he could know about; then at last she went to him and embraced him.

Meanwhile Hermes the guide of souls called together the ghosts of the suitors, rousing them with his golden staff and drawing them whining and gibbering after him. As bats fly about squeaking in the depths of a great cavern when one has fallen from the mass in which they cling, so the ghosts moaned and squealed as Hermes the healer of sorrows led them down into the gloomy dwellings of death. When they had passed the streams of Ocean and the Leucadian Rock, they came to the Gates of the Sun and the land of dreams, and then to the meadows of asphodel where live the shades of those whose labours are finished.

And Odysseus and his family made their peace with the relatives of the suitors, and Odysseus after his long wanderings was once more master in his own house.

VII. CUPID AND PSYCHE

O latest born and loveliest vision far
Of all Olympus' faded hierarchy!

KEATS

THERE was once a king living in the west country who had three daughters, Psyche, the youngest, being so beautiful that citizens and strangers joined in paying her divine honours, half believing her to be a new birth of the love-goddess Venus who once rose from the foaming sea. The people pressed about Psyche as she walked through the town, calling her by the goddess' name and titles and offering her flowery garlands. As her fame spread, travellers came from farther and farther away to see her, until the shrines of Venus, even that at Cythera itself, lay neglected and her altars stood untended and covered with old ashes.

Illustration: Dragon

Venus became angry at this, and swore to be avenged. "What, shall I who am the kindling spirit of all the world share my worship with a mortal girl who must one day die?" She called to her aid her winged son Cupid, who does all kinds of mischief without caring for anyone, and pointed out Psyche to him where she sat in her father's house. "My dear son, I adjure you by a mother's love, punish this disobedient beauty that offends me. Make the girl fall into a desperate passion for the most wretched creature living, something so foul and sick and deformed that nothing can compare with it." So saying, she embraced her son and set off towards the sea, attended by nymphs singing and playing about her.

Psyche meantime, loved by all, nevertheless pined in her unfortunate beauty; for Venus' displeasure kept suitors away from her. She was praised and admired like some painted image, rather than sought as a young woman of flesh and blood. Her two elder sisters were splendidly married to kings, while she sat lonely at home and hated the sad chance that set her apart from the ordinary fate of women. Her father, fearing that some god was the cause of her misfortune, made a journey to an oracle of Apollo, which gave this alarming reply:

> King, lead your daughter to the mountain-side
> Apparelled for her harsh fate like a bride.
> He who shall claim her is no mortal brood,
> But horrid dragon furious and rude
> Who beats the upper air with iron wings,
> Who wearies and breaks down the strongest things.
> He frights great Jove and gods on high that dwell,
> Rivers, and rugged rocks, and shades of Hell.

When they heard the god's answer, the unhappy family spent several days in mourning as the time of the funereal marriage approached. The torches burned with feebly flickering light, the wedding-music was broken by lamentations, the bride

wiped away the tears with her veil; the whole city mourned
with her parents. Psyche reproached them: "When all the
people paid me divine honours, calling me the new Venus, then
you should have wept and grieved for me; now dry your useless
tears and lead me to the place." The people accompanied her
to the top of the mountain where she was to meet her strange
fate, and there they left her. Then when she was left alone,
weeping and trembling on the rock, gentle Zephyr caught her
up with her robes and carried her through the air, setting her
down after some time in a deep valley on a bed of softest
flowers.

Looking about her, Psyche found herself beside a crystal
stream and a green wood, and in the heart of the wood rose a
stately palace, more finely wrought and decorated than the
work of man, shining with precious stones like the light of the
sun. At the pleasant sight Psyche took heart and entered; and
as she walked through the courts and rooms, which all lay
open without lock or bar, she saw many delightful things but
no person at all. When she had seen everything, she heard a
voice that said, "Lady, why do you marvel at these treasures?
All that you see is at your command, and we who speak are
here to serve you; take therefore some rest, and bathe and
refresh yourself, and whatever dishes you care for shall be set
before you when you please." Then Psyche thanked the gods
who watched over her, and refreshed herself as the voice had
said. At table she was served by invisible hands and entertained
by invisible musicians, and all was done for her that she could
desire.

At night Psyche went to the chamber prepared for her and
lay down to sleep; and there after a while someone came to
her, known only by his voice and touch in the darkness. This
was the master of the palace and its treasures, and he greeted
her with great kindness. Night after night he came to her room,
always leaving her again before the morning light.

In this way and with this strange companionship, which became very dear to her, Psyche lived in happiness for many weeks. One night her lover told her that her sisters were searching for her, but that if she heard their lamentations she must pay no attention unless she wished to bring great sorrow on herself and him. Then Psyche remembered her home and family, and suddenly her fine palace seemed to her a prison if she could not speak to her sisters; so she begged and implored him to have them carried to the valley to visit her. At last he gave in to her pleading, but warned her again about taking them into her confidence.

When gentle Zephyr set her dear sisters down in the valley, Psyche made them welcome with great joy, entertaining them with the best the palace could afford. When they saw her happiness and how splendidly she was served, envy took hold in their hearts, and they pressed her for an account of her husband; but she put them off with a tale of his being a fair young man who passed the days hunting on the hills. Then filling their laps with jewels and golden ornaments, she commanded Zephyr to carry them home again.

Away from her their envy at her good fortune increased beyond all measure, and they complained to each other that she was giving herself airs like the consort of a god. Once more Psyche's husband warned her against them, and told her, moreover, that as a testimony of their love she was now carrying his child, who was destined to become one of the immortal gods if only she concealed his secret. Then Psyche was more joyful than before, and loved her husband more dearly than ever.

But those wicked sisters commanded Zephyr to bring them back to the valley, and after congratulating Psyche on the child she would soon bear, they pretended to be concerned for her safety: "for we have learned that he who comes to you every night is a monstrous serpent, who watches over you and caresses you only until your child is born, when he means to devour you both together." Forgetting all the tenderness of her husband, his admonitions and her promises, poor Psyche was very much frightened, and she begged her sisters to advise her in her extremity. Their counsel was to hide a sharp knife and a burning lamp in her room, and at night, after her unknown lover had fallen asleep, to bring out the lamp and strike him by its light. Then having done their work they went away.

At night Psyche made her preparations, trembling still with fear for herself and her unborn child. When her lover slept, she brought out the lamp and carried it towards the bed: and there she saw lying the fair body of her husband, Cupid the god of love himself, still ignorant of her treachery. Now it was with shame and fondness that she trembled, and in her haste to hide the lamp she let a drop of burning oil fall on his shoulder, waking him with the pain. Without a word he caught up his bow and quiver and rose into the air on his white-plumaged wings, flying in a moment far out of sight.

Cupid made his way straight to his mother's chamber, where he lay uneasily waiting for his burned shoulder to heal, enduring Venus' reproaches for flouting her commands. Meanwhile faithful Psyche wandered about searching for him, often weary with her burden but taking no rest. From altar to altar of the lady goddesses she travelled, performing humble services in their temples and imploring their help. Juno, Ceres, all, pitied her repentance and her condition, but none would advise her for fear of the anger of Venus, who of all the divine powers is best able to avenge a slight.

In her distress, Psyche resolved to approach the offended goddess herself, whom she might yet placate by her humility and tears. As she came within sight of the house of Venus, one of the servants ran out and seized her, dragging her by the hair into the presence of the goddess, who beat and struck her and reviled her as a shameless wench. Then she spilled out on the floor a great quantity of wheat, barley, lentils and other grains and ordered her to sort them before night. Psyche did not even begin, but as soon as she was left alone sat down and wept. Immediately an ant, pitying the sorrows of the woman married to a god, called to all her sisters, daughters of the ground that is mother of all, to sort the seeds into separate piles. When the task was done they slipped out of the house and disappeared. But Venus when she came in was furious: "No mortal could have accomplished the task: that scapegrace son of mine must have helped you." She threw her a crust of bread and let her sleep in a corner, while she devised another trial.

In the morning Venus sent Psyche into a thick forest to bring back some golden wool from the fierce sheep that fed there. When Psyche reached the forest, her first thought was to throw herself into the river that ran by and end her griefs; but a green reed on the river-bank, stirred into murmuring music by the wind, whispered to her that this task was an easy one, if only she waited till the heat of the day was past and the sheep came down to the water to drink, leaving tufts of their fleece caught on the bushes. This she could gather and carry back to Venus' house.

Still, when she had done so, Venus accused her of using trickery, and now she set her a harder task yet. From a black rock on top of a high mountain there flowed down a freezing stream whose flow became the dreary Stygian shallows and Cocytus' angry river: with that water she was to fill a crystal vial. The rock proved impossible to climb, and was moreover guarded by crawling dragons that rolled their sleepless bloodshot eyes. As Psyche stood there, cold and rigid like any stone, Jupiter's royal bird the eagle, who had an old obligation to Cupid, swept down on his broad wings and offered to fill her flask as required with the dreadful water of Styx of which the gods themselves are afraid. When Psyche carried it back to

Venus, she was received with worse insults than ever. "You must be a black sorceress, to carry out these tasks and return safely: let us see you perform one more. Take this box and descend to Hell and the house of shadows, and ask Proserpina to send me a little of her beauty: and come back with it as quickly as you can."

At this command Psyche was in the deepest despair. Without pausing even to think of how to carry it out, she hastened up to the top of a high tower intending to throw herself down. Then the tower gave forth a voice and spoke to her: "Wretched woman, do not take the shortest way to Pluto's house and give up your hope of return; but enquire along the roads the path to Taenarus in the waste, where you will find a pit, the breathing-place of Hell. There you can enter, taking in your hands two honey-cakes and in your mouth two pieces of money. On the downward path you will meet people who ask you for help: those you must ignore. At the deadly river, let Charon the ferryman take a coin from your mouth, and he will then carry you over in his rickety boat. As you cross, an old man swimming in the river will hold out to you his rotting hands and cry to you to take him into the boat; but do not heed his crying. When you meet the dog Cerberus that guards the desolate house of death, cast him a honey-cake, and the other one on your return. Proserpina when you enter will make you welcome and offer you a soft seat and delicate foods: be sure that you sit down on the hard ground and accept nothing but a crust of bread. When you have obtained what you came for, go back to the upper world by the way you came. But above all, be careful not to look into the box that Proserpina has filled, nor be too curious about the treasure of the divine beauty."

Psyche immediately made ready for the descent, following the tower's instructions. She passed by in silence all those who would detain her, paid Charon's fee, refused the dead old man in the river, stopped Cerberus' mouth with a honey-cake, and so came into the presence of Proserpina, where she sat down on the hard ground and contented herself with a crust of bread. On her way back, when she had almost reached the house of Venus, she was overcome with a great desire, saying to herself, "Am I not a fool, knowing that I carry the divine beauty, not to take a little of it so that I may please my lover?" And thereupon she opened the box, which seemed to be empty: but a deadly sleep came stealing out of it and covered her face, so that she fell down in the pathway like one dead.

Meanwhile Cupid had recovered from his burn and flown out by the window from the room where Venus thought to keep him shut up, and was now searching to find what had become of his Psyche. When he saw her lying in the path, he wiped the dreadful sleep from her face and put it back in the box, waking her with gentle words. Then he sprang into the air, while Psyche carried to Venus the present of Proserpina.

Won over at last by the long patience of his wife, Cupid flew straight to his father Jupiter to declare his cause. When he had heard all, Jupiter replied with some severity, "My son, you have never treated me so dutifully as you ought, seeing that I am both your father and the lawgiver of the universe: it is your fault that my reputation has been stained by wicked intrigues, to say nothing of transformations at various times into the lowly forms of beasts and birds. However, I will do for you what I can." So saying, he called a council of all the dwellers on high Olympus. He reminded the gods of the wrongs they had suffered at Cupid's hands and from the painful prick of his arrows: now, he said, it was time that the mischievous boy should settle down to a man's responsibilities, and to that end they were gathered together to celebrate his marriage with a virtuous young woman of tried fidelity. Even Venus could not cross the will of great Jove, who pacified her with gracious speeches. Then calling Psyche before him, he gave her to drink the divine nectar, so that she might remain forever with her husband Cupid, ageless and deathless like the immortal gods and honoured like them in the temples and hearts of men.

Now the great marriage-feast was prepared, and Cupid sat at the head of the table with his dear bride in his arms. The Hours had decked all the house with garlands of roses, the Graces perfumed it, the Muses sang sweetly in time to the harping of Apollo their leader, and Venus danced in the midst of them. And when in due time her child was born into happiness and the bright looks of his parents, Psyche named him Pleasure.

VIII

THE PASSING AND
AFTERLIFE OF THE GODS

The oracles are dumb,
No voice or hideous hum
Runs through the archèd roof in
                    words deceiving.
Apollo from his shrine
Can no more divine,
With hollow shriek the steep of
                    Delphos leaving.
No nightly trance or breathèd spell
Inspires the pale-eyed priest from
                    the prophetic cell.

                              MILTON

THE gods of the Greeks and Romans had many ways of making their will known to men. Before any great undertaking, animals were sacrificed and the priests noted their behaviour and searched their bodies for omens. Sometimes the gods sent signs in the form of unexpected natural happenings, as once when Zeus signalled his approval to Odysseus by thundering out of a clear sky. Or a god might send a message in a dream, true or deluding as suited his purpose. Most important, however, certain of the gods had oracles or consulting-places, shrines where people could put questions to the god and obtain

157

answers. At some the questioner slept a night within the holy
precinct, expecting a significant dream. In the sacred oak-grove
of Zeus at Dodona, the priests translated the rustling of the

Delphic priestess on tripod

leaves into messages. At the oracle of Trophonius, named after
a mortal man favoured by Apollo, the suppliant after rigorous
purification descended into a dark and gloomy cave, where he
received his answer in a state of trance.

The most famous of all oracles was that of Apollo at Delphi,
called the centre or navel of the earth. In earlier times it had
belonged not to him but to Mother Earth, for whom it was
guarded by a huge serpent known as the Python. When scarcely

more than a child, Apollo killed the Python with his arrows and seized the shrine, whereupon Earth went to Zeus and demanded justice. She was pacified when Apollo established the Pythian Games in the Python's honour, and when he called the priestess of the shrine the Pythoness after it. When questioned, the Pythoness would seat herself on the tripod and breathe in the vapours that rose from a cleft in the earth. She would then fall into a trance and begin to utter frenzied words, which the priests arranged into rough verses.

Apollo, the god of music and poetry, was also the god of prophecy, which he could pass on as a gift to one whom he especially favoured, as he did to the Trojan princess Cassandra. However, when Cassandra later lost his affection he added the penalty that no one should believe what she said. Thus, though she foresaw the whole fate of Troy and its royal house, she could do nothing to avert it.

> *The angry northern wind*
> *Will blow these sands like Sibyl's leaves abroad.*
>
> SHAKESPEARE

To the Cumaean Sibyl, another woman whom Apollo loved, he promised whatever she might ask. Taking up a handful of dust from the ground, she asked to live as many years as there were grains in her hand; but she forgot to ask for perpetual youth. Apollo offered her this as well if she would grant him her love, and when she refused, he swore that what she had desired should be her punishment. Her destiny was to live for a thousand years in old age and weakness. At last, long after the visit of Aeneas, she shrank to a pitiful heap of skin and bone, and was hung in a bottle from the temple roof. Nothing but her voice was left to her by the Fates. Children playing near the shrine would call out, "Sibyl, what do you want?", and from the bottle a faint chirping voice would answer, "I want to die." Her oracles, in the days when she still gave them, were confused answers written on leaves and tossed up into the wind that swirled about her cave.

When an old woman, this Sibyl came before an early king of Rome named Tarquin the Proud with nine ancient and tattered books of prophecies, which she offered him at a great price. When he refused, she burned three of them in his presence and offered him the remaining six at the same price. He again refused, and now she burned all but three, which she offered him still at the same price. This time Tarquin took the offer. Known as the Sibylline Books, they were kept in the temple of Jupiter on the Capitol Hill and consulted in national emergencies.

> *The lonely mountains o'er,*
> *And the resounding shore,*
> *A voice of weeping heard, and loud lament.*
>
>   MILTON

After many generations the oracles began to decline, and stories were told of how the gods had deserted their holy places. One story, indeed, records the death of a god. A ship on its way from Greece to Italy was passing the island of Paxi when a voice was heard calling "Thamus!", the name of an Egyptian pilot on board. The first and second times Thamus was too astonished to reply, but the third time he called back. Then the voice cried out, "When you come opposite to Palodes, announce there that Great Pan is dead." Thamus half wanted to ignore the mysterious command; but when, opposite Palodes, the wind dropped and all was still, he raised his voice and called towards the land, "Great Pan is dead." Immediately the people on board heard a loud cry of lamentation, as if from a crowd of mourners.

As this took place at about the time when Christ was born, Christian writers made much of the story, because it meant to them the death or overthrow of the old gods at the birth of the new. But the gods did not altogether die; they survived in altered shapes in the stories and traditions of Europe.

> *Canst thou bind the sweet influences of Pleiades, or loose the bands of Orion?*
>
> THE BOOK OF JOB

One place in men's minds where the gods lingered on was in the theory of astrology, or the influence of the stars on human life, now regarded as superstition but once a scientific study. The gods of the Greeks and Romans had originally very little connection with sun, moon, stars, and other natural forces. However, long before the Greeks, the Babylonians had worshipped the sun and moon and the five planets under the names of their great gods, among them the creator-god Marduk and the love-goddess Ishtar. In later times astrological belief spread to Greece and Rome, and the planets began to be called after the Olympian gods who most resembled the Babylonian planetary gods. The names of "the seven stars in the sky" are recalled in those of the days of the week all over Europe, though not always in the same order. Sunday and Monday are called after the sun and moon, and Saturday is Saturn's day. The Latin names of the gods are still to be seen in the French names for the remaining four days: Tuesday is *mardi*, Mars' day; Wednesday *mercredi*, Mercury's day; Thursday *jeudi*, Jove's day; Friday *vendredi*, Venus' day. Our names for these days result from later identification of the classical gods with the gods of the Norsemen. Tuesday belongs to their war-god Tyr, Wednesday to Woden or Odin, the father-god who rules the sky, Thursday to the thunder-god Thor, and Friday to the love-goddess Freya. The correspondence with the classical gods is close but not complete. The Norsemen have no god who resembles Mercury, and they divide Jove's offices of All-Father and thunder-god between Odin and Thor. In German Thursday is not called by a god's name but is *Donnerstag*, the thunder's day.

Each planet ruled on the day called by its name. The planetary powers were supposed to bestow their own characteristics on children born on their own days. That is where we get our adjectives for different kinds of people: "sunny", "lunatic", "martial", "mercurial", "jovial", "venerean" (amorous), "saturnine" (gloomy and sluggish). Some people who regarded the old gods as evil blamed their planets for burdening man with seven deadly sins, respectively: gluttony, envy, wrath, avarice, pride, lust, and sloth.

In the familiar rhyme, "Monday's child is fair of face", the old characteristics can hardly be recognized. But an older version recalls that Monday is the moon's day and Mercury, the patron of merchants, is also the god of thieves. Here he has even stolen the place of his father Jove; for we know from the French day-names that his planet's day is Wednesday.

> Sunday's child is full of grace,
> Monday's child is full in the face,
> Tuesday's child is solemn and sad,
> Wednesday's child is merry and glad,
> Thursday's child is inclined to thieving,
> Friday's child is free in giving,
> And Saturday's child works hard for a living.

A line that most of us know better, "Friday's child is loving and giving", looks back not only to Venus but also to the Christian associations of the day.

Our names for the months of the year are Roman, and four of them come from the names of divinities. March, May and June are called respectively after Mars, Maia the mother of Mercury, and Juno. January is from a Roman god, Janus the guardian of doorways (Latin *ianua*, door), the "opener" of the year. He is always represented with two faces, so that he can look both ways at once.

> *Lo, this is she that was the world's delight.*
>
> SWINBURNE

Long after the decline of classical religion, Venus the love-goddess was said to hold her court in north-eastern Germany under a hill which was called after her the Venusberg or mountain of Venus. Travellers passing after dark would see gleams of torchlight and hear far-off revelry. The goddess herself appeared before the minstrel Tannhäuser and beguiled him into the heart of the hill, where she entertained him splendidly for seven years. At last he sickened of her court with its uninterrupted round of pleasures, and prayed for help to the Virgin Mary; whereupon the side of the hill opened and he came out into the fresh night air. He first took his way to the nearby village church, where he made his confession to the priest and begged to be absolved of the guilt of his seven-years' dallying with the powers of Hell. Horrified by the story, the priest sent him to ask absolution from a higher authority, who also refused him and sent him on. At last he came with his tale before Pope Urban IV, a man renowned for his severity, who drove Tannhäuser away with the words, "Sooner shall the staff in my hand grow green and put out flowers, than that God shall pardon thee!" At that Tannhäuser fell into despair, and he made his way back to the Venusberg, the only place left for a man shut out from Christendom. When he had been gone three days, the Pope's staff grew green and broke into flower. Then Urban sent messengers in search of the minstrel, but as they came up he stepped into the mountain-side, which closed forever behind him.

Such tales show how the gods of the old religion did not die but became the fiends and demons of the new. In goat-horned and goat-footed Satan we may recognize the great god Pan, once the kindly protector of flocks, but now the prince of bogeys. Satan's limp and his connection with subterranean furnaces probably come to him from Vulcan, the Latin form of Hephaestus, the lame smith of the gods. Vulcan's mysterious craft in story often seems somewhat demonic, and like Lucifer he was once thrown out of heaven.

About the fifth century B.C., Zeus' daughter Artemis, the virgin huntress, began to be thought of as the moon. The Romans, who called her Diana, took up this view of her, sometimes depicting her with a crescent moon on her forehead; her brother Phoebus Apollo, the bright-haired archer-god, they explained as the sun. They associated Diana especially with the clear moonlight, and her cousin Hecate and her half-sister Proserpina (Persephone) with the moon's dark or sinister aspects. In European folklore these powers still rule the night: the fairies dance under the protection of Diana, the fairy queen is called Titania (a name of Diana) or Proserpina, and Hecate is the goddess of the witches.

Some of the figures of myth have had a pleasanter afterlife. Apart from her role as a sorceress, Venus lived on as the Queen of Love in the poetry of the Renaissance, and the poets had still more to say about the mischief caused by her arrow-shooting son Cupid. The four sons of Eos, Boreas, Notus, Eurus and Zephyr, can be seen puffing out their cheeks in the corners of old maps. Triton, the fish-tailed conch-blowing son of Neptune (Poseidon), becomes the merman of travellers' tales. The mermaid's origin is more complex. Her dangerously sweet voice recalls the Sirens, while her looking-glass and the

> golden comb
> Wherewith she sits on diamond rocks
> Sleeking her soft alluring locks   (MILTON)

perhaps connect her with Venus and other Mediterranean

love-goddesses who rose from the sea. Saint George's rescue
of a princess from a dragon looks very like Perseus' rescue of
Andromeda, or Hercules' rescue of Hesione. The Pied Piper
who can draw rats by his piping is only one of many magical
musicians whose gifts recall those of Orpheus. Psyche's task of
sorting a heap of seeds occurs in many familiar stories, and
she herself and her mysterious lover meet us again in the tale
of Beauty and the Beast. And where was it that we first met
Endymion, the sleeping shepherd?

> Little boy blue, come blow your horn,
> The sheep's in the meadow, the cow's in the corn.
> Where is the boy who looks after the sheep?
> He's under the haystack, fast asleep.
> Will you wake him? No, not I;
> For if I do, he's sure to cry.

LINES

Here often, when a child, I lay reclined,
I took delight in this locality.
Here stood the infant Ilion of the mind,
And here the Grecian ships did seem to be.
And here again I come, and only find
The drain-cut levels of the marshy lea, –
Grey sandbanks, and pale sunsets, – dreary wind,
Dim shores, dense rains, and heavy-clouded sea.

TENNYSON

FAMILY TREE OF THE OLYMPIANS

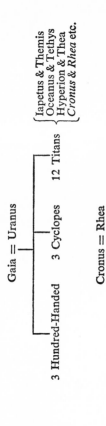

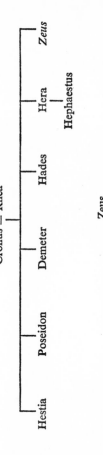

Gaia = Uranus

3 Hundred-Handed   3 Cyclopes   12 Titans

{ Iapetus & Themis
Oceanus & Tethys
Hyperion & Thea
Cronus & Rhea etc. }

Cronus = Rhea

Hestia   Poseidon   Demeter   Hades   Hera   *Zeus*

Hephaestus

Zeus

= [Metis]   = Demeter   = Hera   = Leto   = Maia   = [Semele]

Athene   Persephone   Ares   Apollo & Artemis   Hermes   Dionysus

Pan

FAMILY TREE OF THE ROYAL HOUSE OF THEBES

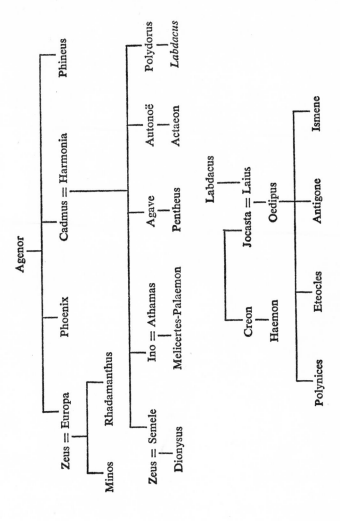

CREATION

> Reign of Uranus (Sky) and Gaia (Earth)

GOLDEN AGE   Reign of Cronus and Titans

SILVER AGE   Reign of Zeus and Olympians . . . .

> Birth of younger Olympians

BRONZE AGE

> Age of ancestors (Europa, Cadmus, Tantalus, etc.) . . . . .

> Age of heroes (Jason, Theseus, Heracles, etc.) . . . . . .

> Fall of Troy to Greeks under Mycenaean king Agamemnon .

IRON AGE   Return of exiled sons of Heracles from the north . . . . .

> Dido receives Aeneas at Carthage . . . .

> Romulus and Remus found Rome . . . .

The Greek myths are told in a sequence which has some relation to the historical sequence of events in the right-hand column. Many of the myths were suggested by the historical events, and where this is the case the two are connected on the chart.

Decline of the oracles and death of Pan . . . .

HISTORY

	NEW STONE AGE
	BRONZE AGE
Great Pyramid and Great Sphinx built in Egypt	B.C. 2500?
Achaean invasions from the north, bringing Olympian religion to Greece	2000-1300
Great age of Mycenaean civilization: founding of Greek city-states	1600-1200
Fall of Minoan empire, destruction of Cnossus; Achaean raids on Crete, Egypt, shores of Black Sea	1400?
Fall of Troy	1184?
Dorian invasion from the north, bringing iron	IRON AGE
Founding of Carthage	814?
Homer, author of *Iliad* and *Odyssey*; Hesiod, author of *Works and Days* and *Theogony*	8th cent.
Founding of Rome	753?
Fall of Jerusalem to Nebuchadnezzar	586
Great age of Athens: tragic dramatists Aeschylus, Sophocles, Euripides	5th cent.
Greeks defeat Persians at Marathon	490
Death of Athenian philosopher Socrates	399
Alexander the Great carries conquests into India	326
Apollonius Rhodius, author of *Argonautica*; Apollodorus, author of *Bibliotheca*	3rd cent.
Beginning of Rome's wars with Carthage	264
Destruction of Carthage by Rome	146
Birth of Vergil, author of *Aeneid* (Latin)	70
Invasion of Britain by Julius Caesar	54
Birth of Ovid, author of *Metamorphoses* (Latin)	43
Probable date of birth of Christ	4
Death of Augustus, first Roman Emperor	A.D. 14
Birth of Apuleius, author of *The Golden Ass* (Latin)	123
Conversion of Constantine, first Christian Roman Emperor	312

171

NOTES

The Illustrations. All the illustrations, with three exceptions, are taken from Greek pottery; for of all the various materials on which the Greeks painted or drew only their baked clay has come down to us in any quantity. It is durable in itself, yet is not so apt to be broken up or melted down for re-use as such stronger substances as marble or bronze.

The earlier or "archaic" vases have their designs painted in black glaze on the reddish Greek clay, giving a silhouette or "black-figured" effect. Page 115 shows a very early example. Often the faces and hands of women are filled in with white, as in the later example by the painter Amasis on page 121: details are scratched into the glaze so that the clay of the vase shows through. Amasis and Exekias are two outstanding Athenian masters of this style, known to us because they signed their work.

Towards the end of the sixth century B.C. a new technique was introduced, the "red-figured", which gradually replaced the black-figured. Figures were now drawn in outline on the clay surface, against a background painted out in black. Red-figured work demanded a finer skill in drawing than black-figured; but it allowed greater freedom of line, as details within the outlines could be applied with pen or brush rather than incised. From the work of Macron, the painter who collaborated with the Athenian potter Hiero, we have taken the red-figured designs on pages 16, 28, and 118.

The three exceptions occur on pages 89, 95, and 165. The first shows a Cretan coin, the second an Egyptian seal. The third is not ancient, but is taken from a mediaeval manuscript copy of Ovid's *Metamorphoses*; the artist has never seen classical painting, and so he draws the gods and goddesses like men and women of his own time.

Further comment on certain illustrations (those on pages 28, 55, 62, 112, 121, 134, and 165) will be found in the notes following.

A Note on Names. Most of the classical myths arose in Greece some centuries before the birth of Christ. In the second century B.C. Greece fell under the power of Rome, and Roman writers began to retell the

Greek stories, altering the names to suit Latin spelling and sometimes changing them to those of their own less colourful gods. Thus Heracles became Hercules, and the sky-god Zeus became Jove or Jupiter. The name "Greece" itself is Latin: the Greeks themselves have always called their country Hellas and its people Hellenes.

It was the Romans who civilized most of Europe, sending in armies, building roads and towns, establishing the rule of law. When the Roman Empire crumbled away, it left in its place the Roman Catholic Church, which continued to use Latin in its services and its books. Roman Catholicism was the religion of the whole of Western Europe until the Protestant Reformation took place in the sixteenth century. Thus Latin remained for centuries the international language of educated Europe, and Greek books and writers were known only in Latin versions. So it comes about that the Latin names of gods and heroes are often more familiar to us than the original Greek ones.

In this book Greek names are used, except in stories in the last two chapters told only by Latin authors. However, Latin spellings have been preferred when these were more familiar: Phoebus and Oedipus instead of Phoibos and Oidipous, Jocasta instead of Iokaste, Circe instead of Kirke. A list of Greek names with their Latin equivalents follows:

Zeus – Jupiter, Jove	*Pan* – Faunus
Poseidon – Neptune	*satyrs* – fauns
Hades – Pluto, Dis	*Cronus* – Saturn
Hera – Juno	*Rhea* – Ops
Demeter – Ceres	*Uranus* – Coelus
Persephone – Proserpina	*Gaia* – Tellus
Dionysus – Bacchus	*Helios* – Sol
Ares – Mars	*Selene* – Luna
Athene – Minerva	*Eos* – Aurora
Artemis – Diana	*Phosphorus* – Lucifer
Hephaestus – Vulcan, Mulciber	*Hesperus* – Vesper
Hermes – Mercury	*Heracles* – Hercules
Aphrodite – Venus	*Asclepius* – Aesculapius
Eros –Cupid	*Hecabe* – Hecuba
Hestia – Vesta	

I. IN THE BEGINNING

These stories are told by several Greek writers, most fully by the early poet Hesiod in his *Theogony*, or Births of the Gods. Hesiod lived, probably in the eighth century B.C., on the slopes of Mount Helicon, where he claimed the Muses taught him his songs as he was tending his sheep. The story of Deucalion and Pyrrha, like that of Phaëthon following, is taken from the Latin poet Ovid. His *Metamorphoses* or Transformations is an elaborate retelling of nearly all the Greek myths and some Roman ones for a sophisticated Roman audience. The poem is bound together by its grand theme of transformation, which the poet sees as the essential process of the universe. Born in 43 B.C., Ovid was a contemporary of the Emperor Augustus.

6 *Eros*: his powers include the physical force of attraction in matter.

7 *adamant*: "invincible". Name given in classical times to the hardest iron and steel, or to diamond.

Cronus: Roman writers explained him as meaning Time, which devours the years as Cronus did his children. This happened through confusion with Greek *chronos*, "time"; and it explains why pictures of Father Time show him carrying Cronus' sickle.

Oceanus: thought of as a great river flowing in a circle round the flat disk of the earth.

nymphs: properly, maiden spirits of waters and springs. Similar spirits are dryads and oreads, attached to trees and mountains. "Nymphs" is frequently used as a general name for all of these.

8 *Morning Star and Evening Star*: both are names of the planet Venus.

Planets: it is later in the classical age, under Babylonian influence, that the planets are given the names of Ares, Hermes, Zeus, Aphrodite, and Cronus (our Mars, Mercury, Jupiter, Venus, and Saturn), and star-worship enters Greek religion. See p. 161.

Saturn: during the Roman feast of Saturnalia held every year in his honour, slaves were waited on by their masters. This reversal of the social order commemorated Saturn's reign when everyone was equal.

Golden Age . . . : archaeology also divides the early history of man into four periods, named after the materials he used in each – the Old Stone, the New Stone, the Bronze and the Iron Ages. ("Archaeology" comes from two Greek words meaning "science of antiquity".) History sees man as working his way up from primitive origins, while mythology usually sees him as progressively falling away from an early happy state. The historical and mythological

Bronze and Iron Ages correspond. Homer, living in the Iron Age, knows that his twelfth-century B.C. heroes did not have the use of iron, and carefully describes their armour, weapons and chariots as bronze.

12 *trident*: a "three-toothed" fishing spear. Britannia on the British penny grasps the trident, symbolizing her rule over the waves.

13 *Hades*: like "the Hesperides", in classical times always the name of a person, never of a place.

14 *the Olympian gods*: once Zeus is established, the names "Mount Olympus" and "heaven" mean the same thing to Greek writers – the abode of the gods.

15 *Lemnos*: like other places pointed out as subterranean workshops of Hephaestus, Lemnos was volcanic. "Volcano" is connected with Hephaestus' Latin name, Vulcan.

invented the lyre: all peoples have stories about the invention of things. In Genesis Jubal and Tubal-Cain are the first musician and the first smith.

lyre: the tortoise-shell is the base, which works as a sound-box. It supports two wooden arms, one on each side, connected at the top with a cross-bar. Seven strings of equal length are stretched between the cross-bar and the shell. These are struck with a plectrum, often as an accompaniment to singing or recitation. A "lyric" poem originally meant one that could be chanted to the accompaniment of the lyre.

16 *satyrs*: associated with Pan in art and legend are wild men with animal parts like goats' legs and horns or horses' tails, living among woods and hills. The Latin name for Pan is Faunus, for the satyrs *fauni*. From the Latin goddesses of wild life and flowers we get our words "fauna" and "flora".

17 *"his vulture"*: Byron in this poem on the career of Napoleon is thinking, not of the royal bird of Zeus, but of the two vultures who tear at the liver of Tityus, another ambitious giant punished by Zeus. The ancient authors themselves quite often combine two stories in this way.

20 *"the unwiser son of Japhet"*: Milton, writing in the mid-seventeenth century, is following the historians of his day in trying to relate the figures of classical mythology to those of the Bible, here the Titan Iapetus and the third son of Noah. The person he is comparing to Pandora is Eve.

23 *chest*: another floating box appears in the story of Perseus (p. 55).
The Latin word for "chest" is *arca*: hence our word "Ark" for the
vessel in which Noah survived the Flood.

25 *Helios, Heliades*: the sun-god gives his name to a chemical element,
helium. Heliades means "children of Helios", here his daughters.
Similarly, the Hesperides are the daughters of Hesperus; Alcides,
a name of Heracles, means "grandson of Alcaeus"; and Agamemnon is sometimes called Atreides after his father Atreus. Names
like these indicating parentage or ancestry are called "patrony-
mics".

Phaëthon: the phaeton, a four-wheeled light carriage drawn by two
horses, was named after him. This story is one of many dealing
with a rash promise or repented wish or curse: compare Theseus'
curse on Hippolytus (p. 92). The theme reflects the belief of
primitive peoples in the magically binding power of words. The
god who broke an oath sworn by Styx forthwith lay unconscious
for a year and for the next nine years was banished from heaven.

27 *Scorpion and Crab*: Scorpio and Cancer, two of the twelve constellations making up the Zodiac or path of the sun through the
sky. "Zodiac", like "zoölogy", is related to Greek *zoös*, "living".

II. SPRING AND WINTER

The story of Demeter and Persephone is told best in an early Greek
poem known as the "Homeric Hymn to Demeter", though no longer
thought of as Homer's work. The tale of the wandering goddess is older
still than Greek mythology, going back to Egypt and the search of Isis
for her lost husband Osiris. Ovid tells the stories of Adonis, Hyacinthus,
Narcissus and Orpheus in his *Metamorphoses*.

28 *Demeter, Triptolemus, Persephone (illustration)*: Triptolemus,
Demophoön's older brother, is said to have been sent forth in a
chariot by Demeter, to carry seed-corn and the art of its cultivation
to distant countries.

29 *narcissus*: probably the yellow daffodil. A sinister flower in mythology, its name is connected with *narke*, "numbness", from which
we get "narcotic".

30 *Eleusis*: a town near Athens where an elaborate festival called the
Eleusinian Mysteries was celebrated every autumn in honour of
Demeter and her daughter. Probably one of the intentions of this

story was to explain Demeter's connection with Eleusis.

35 *Sabaea*: the biblical Sheba, whose Queen brought gold and spices to Solomon.

38 *"his lute"*: a guitar-like stringed instrument of Shakespeare's time, replacing in the poem the classical lyre.

39 *Ixion, Sisyphus*: impious men condemned to endless suffering in Tartarus, the underworld place of punishment. Ixion, a friend of the gods and a guest at their table, repaid their hospitality by attempting to carry off Hera, and was punished by being bound to a fiery wheel. Sisyphus, who betrayed a secret of Zeus, had forever to keep pushing a heavy stone uphill, which never reached the top but always kept rolling down again. Other sufferers in Tartarus were Tantalus (p. 124); Tityus (p. 175); the fifty Danaids (daughters of Danaus), who for murdering their husbands were forced incessantly to try to carry water in sieves, or jars with holes in the bottom.

40 *Arion, Sappho, Alcaeus*: the earliest Greek lyric poets whose writings have survived. We know almost nothing about their lives, but legends grew up around all three. Sappho, a woman, was sometimes called "the tenth Muse". Arion, thrown overboard by sailors, is said to have been carried triumphantly ashore by dolphins, who were delighted by his performance on the lyre.

III. LOVES OF THE GODS AND METAMORPHOSES

All the stories told in this chapter are from Ovid's *Metamorphoses* and are best known in his versions.

42 *Arcas*: the supposed ancestor of the Arcadians, as Phoenix was of the Phoenicians and Romulus of the Romans. A man who gives his name to a race, or more likely is invented to explain its name, is called its "eponym".

Arcturus: "the bear-guard", a star in the constellation Boötes, next to the Great Bear. In other accounts Arcas became the constellation of the Little Bear, whose tail contains the Pole Star, by which early sailors steered. The sailors' name for the Pole Star and its constellation, Cynosure, literally "dog's tail", comes to mean in English "a centre of attention".

Egyptians: the Greeks, who unlike the Egyptians did not worship animal-formed or animal-headed deities, explained the Egyptian cow-goddess Hathor, a form of the great goddess Isis, as the transformed maiden Io.

45 *the boy Eros*: in the story of the creation told by Hesiod, Eros ("Love", in Latin, Cupid) was brought forth in the beginning by Night and Erebus, and thus is almost the oldest of the gods. Later writers, though, make him the youngest, the child of Aphrodite, an eternally mischievous little boy wounding men and gods alike with his arrows. In the Roman story of Cupid and Psyche, told near the end of this book, Love begins to grow up.

46 *Arachne*: this story, like some that follow, is "aetiological": that is, it is told to give the "cause" of something, here the spider's nature. Modern examples would be some of Kipling's *Just-So Stories*, like "How the Leopard got his Spots". Sometimes aetiological stories explain ritual, like Hesiod's tale of why men burn bones for the gods, p. 17.

IV. THE HEROES

These tales of the heroes before the Trojan War are all told briefly by Ovid in the *Metamorphoses*, and at greater length by a late Greek writer, Apollodorus, born about 180 B.C., in his *Bibliotheca*, or Library, a survey of Greek mythology. The fifth-century B.C. tragic dramatists Sophocles and Euripides used incidents from the lives of Heracles, Jason and Theseus in their plays. The history of Jason is told most fully by the Alexandrian poet Apollonius Rhodius in his epic *The Argonautica*, written in Greek in the third century B.C.

55 *Gorgon shield (illustration)*: Greek shields were decorated, often with Gorgon faces to frighten enemies. Gorgon masks were attached also to ovens, foundries and house-chimneys to scare off evil spirits.

58 *Andromeda, Cassiopeia*: the stories do not agree as to whether it was of her own or her daughter's beauty that Cassiopeia boasted. Milton calls her "starred" because the adventure is recorded in the names of a group of northern constellations: Cassiopeia, Andromeda, Cepheus (Andromeda's father), Perseus, Cetus ("Seamonster"), and Pegasus, the winged horse said to have sprung from Medusa's body at her death.

59 *cross-legged*: this is "sympathetic magic", the attempt to produce

a certain effect by imitating it – bring rain by scattering water, injure an enemy by wounding an image of him. In some places the belief still lingers that a baby cannot be born or a soul part from ·its body in a house where there are doors locked or knots tied.

60 *purification*: a murderer, whether man or god, had to undergo a ritual of purification, sometimes with a penalty of exile, before he could return to society. Apollo, who saw to this law's being carried out, himself submitted to purification and exile twice: for the deaths of the Python (p. 159) and of the Cyclopes (p. 64). The ritual required the sacrifice of a ram or pig, probably as a substitute for the blood of the murderer.

61 *Cup of the Sun*: the vessel in which the sleeping Sun was carried over the sea every night from west to east.

pillars: our dollar sign $ may come from the symbol on old Spanish dollars of the Pillars of Hercules decked with garlands by sailors setting out across the unknown western sea, or rejoicing in their return.

62 *Heracles in the Cup of the Sun (illustration)*: the hero carries his club and bow, and wears the head of his lion-skin as a helmet.

63 *"Alcides"*: a patronymic: see note to p. 25, *Heliades*.

68 *Euxine Sea*: "friendly to strangers", now more suitably called the Black Sea. Like the "Eumenides" (p. 126) and the "Pacific" Ocean, the "Euxine" is a complimentary, not a descriptive, title.

70 *Castor and Polydeuces*: they were later changed into the constellation Gemini, the Heavenly Twins. Perhaps because of their voyage in the Argo, they were the protectors of sailors. Another name of theirs is the Dioscuri, or "sons of Zeus".

73 *sacrifice*: for the Olympians, a white victim, usually an ox, was killed on an altar with its throat upward. The inedible parts were burned for the gods, while the worshippers ate the meat (see p. 17 for an explanation of this custom). For the powers of earth or the underworld the victim, usually a black ram or pig, was killed with its throat downwards, bleeding or falling into a pit. The worshipper took none of the meat, the carcass being usually destroyed in a "holocaust" or wholesale burning. This type of sacrifice, performed also at funerals to honour the dead, was carried out at night.

78 *suppliant*: an exile or stranger claiming shelter or asylum at a temple sat down by the altar. In a private house he sat by the hearth, the centre of family life and worship. Suppliants like other

strangers were under the special protection of Zeus.

79 *Sirens*: two or three in number, like the Harpies they had the heads
of maidens and the bodies of birds. In later times they were thought
of as fish-tailed, like our mermaids.

Scylla and Charybdis: Charybdis was a whirlpool, Scylla a dangerous rock, the home of a dog-headed, man-eating hag.

86 *aconite*: a poison extracted from the plant monk's-hood or wolf's-
bane.

87 *Minotaur*: literally, "Minos-bull". This is probably a story told to
explain some features of Cretan religious ritual, in which, to judge
from excavated seals, vase-paintings and murals, both bulls and
labyrinths had a central place.

Daedalus: the supposed inventor of carpentry, and of several
devices including the saw, the axe, the plumb-line, the augur, and
glue, also life-sized automata, or robots. His name means "skilful", and from it comes English "daedal", meaning manifold or
mysterious.

88 *labyrinth*: a Greek word meaning "maze". The original labyrinth
of the story may have been the immense and complicated palace
at Cnossus in Crete, already in ruins when Greek civilization
began, and excavated in the twentieth century by Sir Arthur Evans.
The ancient Cretan Bronze Age culture, which collapsed from unknown causes in about 1400 B.C., is called after its legendary king
"Minoan".

90 *clew*: literally, a ball of thread. From its use in this tale comes the
meaning usually attached to its other spelling, "clue".

93 *Nemi*: so called from the grove, Latin *nemus*.

bough of gold: this reappears in the story of Aeneas (p. 128). One
of the most influential books of modern times, Sir James G.
Frazer's *The Golden Bough*, explains the bough as mistletoe with
its yellow berries growing on the oak. Surveying the whole field of
European folk-lore, Frazer attempts to account for the strange
custom of Nemi.

V. THE ROYAL HOUSE OF THEBES

These stories are told by several Greek writers, and by Ovid in the
Metamorphoses. Euripides, in the fifth century B.C., told the story of
Pentheus in his tragedy *The Bacchae* – "women followers of Bacchus",

or Dionysus. Sophocles composed a series of four plays about the later troubles of Thebes: *Oedipus the King, Oedipus at Colonus, The Seven Against Thebes,* and *Antigone.*

96 *Tyre*: with Sidon and Byblus, one of the great seacoast cities of Phoenicia, already a powerful trading nation before the rise of Greece. Its valuable export was the purple dye from the *murex*, a shellfish, which became a sign of rank throughout the Mediterranean world.

Cadmus: he was said to have carried the alphabet to Greece. His father Agenor, a great-grandson of Io (p. 42), came to Tyre from Egypt, and Cadmus' brother Phoenix became the ancestor of the Phoenicians. Though historians do not now believe that Thebes, which Cadmus was said to have founded, was a Phoenician colony, it is certain that the Greek alphabet is descended from the Phoenician, and possible that Phoenician script itself came from Egypt.

100 *thyrsus*: staff tipped with a pine-cone, an emblem of Dionysus. From it comes the pine-cone design we sometimes see in lacework patterns or in the stonework on buildings. Artists who forget its origin make it look like a pineapple.

Teiresias: like most poets and prophets of Greek myth, a blind man gifted with inner sight. Compare Phineus (p. 70) and Demodocus (p. 141). As a punishment for offending the gods, Teiresias spent some years as a woman, and had thus gained complete human experience.

102 *Sphinx*: most of the hybrid monsters of Greek mythology come originally from the East. The best-known sphinx is the immense stone one, lion-bodied and human-headed (but without wings), that guards the Nile Valley at Gizeh in Egypt. The Great Sphinx, as it is called, is one of the earliest works of Egyptian civilization, which began at least two thousand years before that of Greece.

103 *kingdom*: the Greek hero who wins a kingdom, even if he is the true heir, regularly comes to it after long wanderings and the withstanding of some great ordeal. As in fairy-tales, he often receives with the kingdom the hand of a princess. This has suggested to some that in early European societies the ruling power was inherited by the women of the royal house, not the men, who acquired it only by marriage to one of them. This institution, where a king rules less in his own right than as the queen's consort, is called "matriarchy". One might compare the position of Arete (p. 140).

VI. THE TALE OF TROY

The histories of the Trojan War and the return of Odysseus are told by the earliest and most famous of Greek poets, Homer, in the two great Greek epics, the *Iliad* – "the matter of Ilion", or Troy, and the *Odyssey* – "the matter of Odysseus". Nothing definite is known of Homer's life. He lived some time before 700 B.C.: his name means "hostage", suggesting a prisoner or slave, and tradition makes him a blind bard like his own Demodocus (p. 141), singing his lays at the courts of princes. Homer does not tell the stories of the apple of discord and the homecoming of Agamemnon: these are taken respectively from *The Trojan Women* by the fifth-century B.C. dramatist Euripides, and from the *Oresteia* by his contemporary Aeschylus, a cycle of three plays about the house of Atreus: *Agamemnon, The Libation-Bearers,* and *The Eumenides.* The wanderings of Aeneas, the ancestor of the Romans, are the subject of the greatest of Latin poems, Vergil's *Aeneid* (unfinished at his death in 19 B.C.), the epic of the founding and destiny of Rome. Vergil and Apollonius Rhodius drew largely on Homer in their epics: this is one reason why the adventures of Aeneas and Jason often closely resemble those of Odysseus.

105 *Troy*: situated in Phrygia in Asia Minor beside the entrance of the Hellespont (modern Dardanelles) from the Aegean. Heinrich Schliemann, excavating in 1873 on the site of the modern Turkish village of Hissarlik, unearthed not just Homer's Troy but a series of nine cities built each on the ruins of its predecessor, stretching in time from before 2500 B.C. to after the reign of the Roman Emperor Constantine (died 337 A.D.). Homer's Troy was the seventh of these cities: Troy VII had a strong wall with watchtowers and three gates, and was destroyed by fire at about the date traditionally assigned to Troy's overthrow by the Greeks – 1184 B.C.

107 *Mycenae*: Agamemnon was the overlord of the Argive district of the Peloponnesus, whose principal cities were Argos, Mycenae and Tiryns. These last two were among the oldest of Greek cities, being centres of Minoan civilization (see note to p. 88). Mycenae, excavated by Schliemann in 1875, is famous for its Lion Gate, its nine "beehive" tombs – Schliemann called the largest "the Treasury of Atreus" – , and the immense hoard of finely-worked gold articles buried with its princes.

109 *lay siege to the city*: not a siege in the modern sense, with the city

surrounded and its defenders starving. The Trojans were able to keep up their trade with the hinterland, while the Greeks bought supplies along the seacoast and from the islands. Consequently the war could go on indefinitely.

112 *The weighing of dooms (illustration)*: the artist has shown Hermes holding the scales in place of Zeus, probably because he thinks of Hermes as revealing to men on earth what takes place in heaven.

113 *doom*: what Zeus weighs are two *keres thanatoio*, "dooms of death", one for each of the heroes. A *ker* is a small winged sprite, the bearer sometimes of good but usually of evil. The ills that flew out of Pandora's box – griefs, diseases, old age and death – were a swarm of *keres*, and Hope too was a *ker*. The *ker* that Zeus weighs for each of the heroes is that hero's own impending death, and Hector's sinks down because his fate is upon him. Zeus is using his scales to ascertain what outcome the Fates have decreed. He is not using them to decide the contest itself, as our expression "His fate hangs in the balance" might suggest.

120 *The Returns*: "Nostoi", the name the Greeks themselves gave to these tales of the aftermath of Troy. Hence English "nostalgia", homesickness or longing for the past, from *nostos*, homecoming, and *algos*, pain.

121 *Athene and Poseidon (illustration)*: Athene's upper garment is her *aegis* or short goat-skin cloak. It is edged sometimes with curly tufts of goat's-hair, sometimes as here with curling snakes.

122 *ambrosia*: meaning "immortal", "divine", ambrosia is the food of the gods as nectar is their drink.

123 *Elysian fields*: a happy place, sometimes called the Isles of the Blessed, where certain especially favoured heroes enjoy an immortal life after death. It was sometimes thought of as in the far west, otherwise as part of the underworld realm of Hades.

"Tragedy": the Greek tragic dramatists, Aeschylus, Sophocles and Euripides, took the subjects of their greatest plays from the histories of Thebes (Oedipus and his children) and the house of Atreus or Pelops (Agamemnon's family).

124 *Pelops*: he gives his name to the Peloponnesus, "Isle of Pelops", the peninsular southern half of Greece, joined to the mainland by the Isthmus of Corinth.

125 *Areopagus*: "the hill of Ares", just outside Athens, where the court of justice was held. It is called after Ares because he committed a

murder and became the first man tried there. This is "Mars' Hill" where St. Paul preached to the Athenians (Acts xvii. 22).

125 *child, parent*: Apollo is here the spokesman of a new principle. In early times the Greeks like other peoples traced descent through the female line, which was easier to establish than the male. Thus a son's first responsibility would be to his mother as his nearest kin. The Furies' accusation of Orestes rests on this old order of things. At some time a switch to emphasis on the male line – "patriliny" rather than "matriliny" – took place, probably under the influence of the new Olympian religion if not exactly by a god's decree. Greek religion as we know it, dominated by Zeus the All-Father, is male-centred. But before an invading people brought in the worship of the Olympians, the Greeks seem to have been much more concerned, like most of their Mediterranean neighbours, with female powers such as Mother Earth.

Acropolis: "high point of the city", citadel. Ancient cities usually began as fortified hill-tops and spread outwards: temples and palaces would later occupy the central height. The Athenian Acropolis is crowned with a group of buildings that is still one of the wonders of Europe, constructed in the fifth century B.C. from the local white marble. Chief among these is the Parthenon, the temple of "the virgin" (Athene).

126 *Trojan princes*: these were numerous King Priam, an oriental-style monarch with a harem, had fifty sons. Hecabe, his chief wife, was the mother of Hector. Aeneas belonged to the younger branch of the Trojan royal house: his great-great-grandfather Tros – hence "Troy" – was also Hector's. Not only the Romans were anxious to trace their ancestry to Troy. The English in the Middle Ages believed that their island was settled by Aeneas' descendant Brutus and took from him its name of Britain.

127 *Carthage*: a colony of the great trading city of Tyre in Phoenicia, founded about 814 B.C. in North Africa – some 250 years too late to shelter Aeneas as he fled from Troy. Vergil, who tells the story, is not pretending to write history when he suggests a background for the later troubles between Carthage and Rome.

128 *doves*: these were sacred to Aphrodite and were said to draw her chariot through the air. The eagle was sacred to Zeus and the peacock to Hera. Through its association with Athene, the owl, figured on the coins of her city, became the traditional bird of wisdom.

128 *Tartarus*: sometimes used for the whole realm of Hades, but properly the underworld place of punishment, inhabited by the great sinners, Tantalus, Sisyphus and the rest.

134 *Circe (illustration)*: the Greeks always mixed their wine with water in a bowl before drinking it.

135 *herald's staff*: the *caduceus*, carried by Greek heralds and ambassadors as a mark of their office. That of Hermes had two serpents twined round it, their heads meeting at the top, and in late classical art was surmounted by a small pair of wings as a symbol of his speed. It is not to be confused with the staff of Asclepius, the patron of medicine, about which twines a single snake. Hermes' staff had magical powers: it could lull people to sleep, and also controlled the souls of the dead, which it was Hermes' duty to lead to the underworld. Hermes is also recognized by winged boots and a traveller's broad-brimmed hat, sometimes also winged.

Persephone's country: the early Greeks had two conceptions of the abode of the dead: that it was underground, and that it was a country in the farthest west, the direction of the setting sun. In the *Odyssey* these traditions are combined: the entrance to the house of Hades is in "Persephone's country" in the west, where the ghosts come up when they are summoned.

ghosts of the dead: the afterlife imagined by the Greeks was a joyless, shadowy affair. The ghosts were the merest phantoms, without strength and without understanding, lacking the blood that is the vigour of living men. They were objects of pity, but hardly of fear. Homer speaks with respect in this passage of "the glorious tribes of the dead", but again in almost the same breath he calls them "the weak heads of the dead".

140 *palace washing*: most Homeric kings, with a few exceptions like Agamemnon, were very petty rulers indeed – the chief men of their districts, comparable to English squires. Conditions of life in that age did not allow even royalty to be idle: princesses washed, princes like Anchises tended cattle, queens spun and wove. Mediterranean women in country places still trample their wash in stone cisterns built in the paths of streams.

144 *two gates*: while horn cut thin enough is transparent, ivory is opaque, therefore perhaps deluding. The Greeks, like the Egyptians, from very early times brought ivory in from Ethiopia.

147 *dwellings of death*: the Leucadian Rock was a mythical landmark

beyond the western sea. The Gates of the Sun were those by which the sun-god Helios descended every night to commence his journey under the earth back to his eastern point of rising. The land of dreams was said to be either a part of the underworld or situated beside its entrance. The realm of the dead, ruled by Hades and Persephone, was a dreary plain covered with asphodel, a common Mediterranean weed, colourless, dry and crackling. Our "daffodil" comes from "asphodel": though actually different flowers, they belong to the same family.

VII. CUPID AND PSYCHE

Only one author gives this story: Apuleius, in the course of his Latin prose novel, *The Golden Ass*, written late in the second century A.D. There it is told by an old woman in a robbers' den to a kidnapped maiden, to pass the time. We have no way of knowing whether Apuleius found the story or invented it. In many ways it is more like the fairy-tales of mediaeval Europe than like the older classical myths. The names of its hero and heroine are suggestive: Cupid, in Greek Eros, is the god of Love, and *psyche*, the Greek word for "butterfly", also means "soul".

154 *the breathing-place of Hell*: in the later classical age many barren or dreary regions, not necessarily in the far west, were thought of as entrances to the underworld. In Taenarus in the Peloponnesus was the cave through which Heracles was said to have dragged up Hades' watchdog Cerberus. Lake Avernus (p. 128) had another such entrance-cavern, through which Aeneas descended with the Sibyl. Poisonous vapours pouring from its mouth helped its infernal reputation: Vergil derives its name from Greek *a-ornos*, "bird-less".

two pieces of money: the Greeks buried their dead with an obol (a small coin) in the mouth as Charon's fee. Psyche takes two coins, as she will make the crossing twice.

accept nothing: just as Psyche would have put herself in danger had she stopped to help those who asked her, so by accepting from Proserpina more than was strictly necessary she would have given Proserpina power over her. Proserpina herself became bound to the underworld by accepting the pomegranate offered her there by Pluto, Greek Hades, (p. 34).

155 *a great desire*: what helps to make this story so like a fairy-tale is its insistence on magical prohibitions: the lover who must not be looked at, the box that must not be opened. Examples in other stories are Pandora's box (p. 20), the bag of the winds (p. 132), and Hades' command to Orpheus not to look back at his wife (p. 39). Like Adam and Eve, heroes and heroines always break these conditions: otherwise there would be no story.

156 *Hours*: goddesses of the seasons, concerned with the fertility of the earth. They were sometimes three, sometimes four, and had different names in different places.

Graces: the three daughters of Zeus and Eurynome, called Charites by the Greeks, embodying qualities of grace, beauty and charm. They do little in mythology but wait on the love-goddess. Names: Aglaia, Euphrosyne, Thalia.

Muses: daughters of Zeus and Mnemosyne (Memory), patronesses of poetry and of music, which takes its name from them. "Music" is "that which belongs to the Muses", and a "museum" is a "place of the Muses". They are nine in number, and their haunts are all mountains – Boeotian Mount Helicon, where they appeared to Hesiod, with its sacred spring Hippocrene; Mount Pierus in Pieria, where they were born; and Phocian Mount Parnassus, at whose foot was Apollo's oracle of Delphi. Apollo, the god of poetry, is their leader and plays for their dances on his lyre. The Romans assigned specific functions to the Muses according to their traditional names: Calliope was the Muse of epic poetry, Clio of history, Euterpe of flute-music, Terpsichore of the dance, Erato of lyric poetry, Melpomene of tragedy, Thalia of comedy, Polyhymnia of rhetoric, and Urania of astronomy.

VIII. THE PASSING AND AFTERLIFE OF THE GODS

158 *centre of the earth*: the story was that Zeus had released two eagles, one from the eastern edge of the world and one from the western, and that they met at Delphi. The oracle possessed a sacred rock known as the *omphalos* or navel.

159 *Pythian Games*: a festival held regularly at Delphi, consisting of athletic contests but more importantly of "musical" competitions, in instrumental music, singing, drama, and verse and prose recitations. These events were held in honour of Apollo, and were second in importance only to the Olympic Games, celebrating Olympian

Zeus, held at Olympia in the western district of Elis and consisting entirely of athletic events. Victors in the Pythian Games were crowned with wreaths of bay leaves (also called laurel) cut in the nearby Vale of Tempe; Olympic victors, with wild olive.

159 *tripod*: "three-legged", the stool on which the priestess sat.

160 *Capitol Hill*: one of the seven hills on which Rome was built. Its name is said to mean Hill of the Head, from a bleeding human head found by workmen laying the temple's foundations.

161 *"Pleiades", "Orion"*: the English Bible uses the Greek names of these constellations. The Pleiades were the seven daughters of Atlas, taking their name from their mother, Pleione. Orion, the great hunter, pursued them for five years; and the chase never ended, but was translated by the gods to the heavens. Orion became a constellation and the sisters a cluster of seven stars near by. One of the seven was Maia, the mother by Zeus of Hermes.

164 *Diana*: other names the poets give to Diana as moon-goddess are Luna, Latin "moon"; Phoebe, the feminine of Phoebus; Titania, the feminine of Titan, a title of the sun; Cynthia, from her birthplace, Mount Cynthus in Delos. Early Greek mythology had a moon-goddess, Selene, and a sun-god, Helios, though never very important. The later writers retell their stories, making Diana, and not Selene, the goddess who loved Endymion, and making Apollo the father of Phaëthon in place of Helios.

Hecate: one of the ancient female powers of older Greek mythology. She may have once been very important: Hesiod says that Zeus gave her power "in earth and sea and sky". In historical times she was a minor goddess, always associated with darkness, magic and the underworld. To her belonged cross-roads, places where a road was joined by a side-path, where her image might be set up with three faces to look in all three directions. The Romans called her Hecate Trivia, "of three ways", and thus she became known as a "triple goddess". When she was later identified with the dark of the moon, and writers had forgotten why she was triple in the first place, they connected her with Diana and Proserpina to make up the three phases of the moon.

165 *The sleeping shepherd (illustration)*: this is actually a French mediaeval illustration to the tale of Hermes and Argus. Both are dressed as peasants, and Hermes plays, instead of the classical shepherd's pipe, a simple form of bagpipe.

Pronouncing and Descriptive
INDEX

A Note on Pronunciation. We are not certain how the Greeks or Romans pronounced every sound in their language. Moreover, just as the spelling of many names has become anglicized by use, so too has the pronunciation. There is therefore some choice in pronunciation as well as in spelling.

In the index long vowels only have been marked. All other vowels are either short or diphthongs. The accented syllable is marked ' . Two vowels with a diaeresis are pronounced separately (e.g., Alci' no-üs).

Vowels: long vowels are pronounced: Ā (*make*), Ē (*make* or *feet*), Ī (*feet* or *fine*), Ō (*low*), Ū (*duly*), Ȳ (*type*).

short vowels are pronounced: A (*mat*), E (*let*), I (*fit*), O (*dot*), U (*rut*), Y (*myth*).

Consonants: CH is always pronounced *k*. Greek and Latin know only the hard pronunciations of C and G, as in *cat* and *get*; but in English we often soften G before *e*, and C before *e*, *i*, and *y*.

Diphthongs: AE (*feet*), OE (*feet*), AI (*fine*), EI (*may* or *feet*) are diphthongs unless indicated otherwise. EU as a diphthong is pronounced as *you*, but can ordinarily be separated (e.g., Zeus is always one syllable, but Orpheus, Theseus may be pronounced Or' phe-us, Thē' se-us if preferred).

189

SOURCES OF QUOTATIONS

title-page John Milton, *Comus*, 513-19.
page 6 John Milton, *Paradise Lost*, I. 9-10.
  8 Edmund Spenser, *The Faery Queen*, V. 9.
  10 Robert Browning, "Imperante Augusto Natus Est—".
  13 John Milton, "At a Vacation Exercise".
  17 George Gordon, Lord Byron, "Ode to Napoleon Buonaparte".
  20 John Milton, *Paradise Lost*, IV. 714-19.
  21 John Milton, *Paradise Lost*, XI. 10-14.
  25 Andrew Marvell, "The Nymph Complaining for the Death of her Fawn".
  28 John Milton, *Paradise Lost*, IV. 268-72.
  35 John Milton, *Comus*, 998-1002.
  36 John Milton, "On the Death of a Fair Infant".
  37 Edmund Spenser, *The Faery Queen*, III. vi. 45.
  38 William Shakespeare, *Henry VIII*, III. i.
  41 William Shakespeare, *The Winter's Tale*, IV. iii. 25-30.
  44 John Lyly, *Midas*, IV. i. 103-8.
  44 Andrew Marvell, "The Garden".
  45 Thomas Moore, "Believe me if all those endearing young charms".
  46 William Shakespeare, *The Merchant of Venice*, V. i. 109-10.
  46 Edmund Spenser, "Muiopotmos".
  47 Richard Barnefield, "As it fell upon a day".
  49 William Shakespeare, *The Merchant of Venice*, III. ii. 101-2.
  51 John Milton, "On the Morning of Christ's Nativity".
  52 Alexander Pope, *The Rape of the Lock*, III. 121-4.
  53 Ovid, *Metamorphoses*, VIII. 722-4 (translated by John Dryden).
  55 John Fletcher, "Hear, ye ladies".
  56 John Milton, *Comus*, 447-9.
  57 John Milton, "Il Penseroso".
  59 William Shakespeare, *Love's Labour's Lost*, V. ii. 589-92.
  60 Edmund Spenser, *The Faery Queen*, I. xi. 27-9.
  62 William Shakespeare, *Pericles*, I. i. 26-8.
  63 John Milton, *Paradise Regained*, IV. 563-8.
  64 John Milton, "On His Deceased Wife".